Radio Man

Radio Man

✦

Marconi Sahib

Mahrie Locket

iUniverse, Inc.

New York Lincoln Shanghai

Radio Man
Marconi Sahib

Copyright © 2007 by Mahrie Locket

iUniverse books may be ordered through booksellers or by contacting:

iUniverse
2021 Pine Lake Road, Suite 100
Lincoln, NE 68512
www.iuniverse.com
1-800-Authors (1-800-288-4677)

Because of the dynamic nature of the Internet, any Web addresses or links contained in this book may have changed since publication and may no longer be valid.

The views expressed in this work are solely those of the author and do not necessarily reflect the views of the publisher, and the publisher hereby disclaims any responsibility for them.

ISBN: 978-0-595-47022-8 (pbk)
ISBN: 978-0-595-91306-0 (ebk)

Printed in the United States of America

Readers will notice that the diary contains many references that are no longer in use, and many in today's society find offensive. This includes what would now be considered racial slurs, or insensitive to minorities.

In publishing this work, I agonized over whether to edit the diary to conform to modern standards, or to publish verbatim. In the end, I left the diary intact, so as to both authentically represent Alan, and the society in which he lived. In so doing, we do not in any way wish to offend anyone, rather we seek to show the reader the world in which Alan lived, with all its imperfections.

This book is dedicated to Alan K.M. Patterson

and the British Merchant Marine Service

(A.K.M.P 1914–1994)

Contents

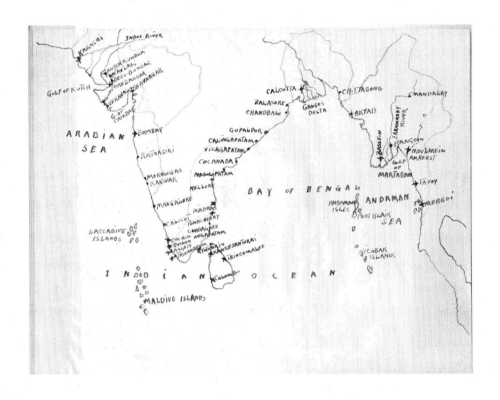

Map was hand-sketched by Alan Patterson in 1938

The Merchant Service Bum

You've seen him on the street
Rolling round on groggy feet
You've despised him when he's been out on a spree
On a dark and lonely ship
Through a submarine and mine infested sea.

You have cheered the navy lads
On their heavy ironclads:
You can spare a cheer for Tommy Atkins too.
You may have a touch of funk
When you read "Big mail boat sunk",
Did you think of the merchant service crew.

You have mourned about the cost
Of every vessel lost-
It has put you in a pessimistic mood.
But you never said "Well Done!"
Or congratulated one,
Who helps to bring your wife and kiddies food.

He has brought your wounded home
Through a mine infested zone
He has ferried all your troops to France by night.
He belongs to no brigade,
Is neglected, underpaid—
Yet is often in the thickest of the fight.

He has fought the lurking hun
With an ancient four inch gun;
And he's done his bit to get them on the run.
Yet you've never heard him boast
To the folks that need him most …
In fact he's rather reticent and glum.

Wouldn't you feel that way too, If, no matter what you do,
You're still another merchant service bum?
He can collar huns and smite'em
To the real "Ad infinitum'"
And as for wops he doesn't give a damn
His social standing's nil and you regard him as a pill,
But you've got to hand it to him.… He's a man.

Written by one of us who has since lost his life by enemy action.

Prologue

I was born March 8th, 1914, in a rather bleak looking farm house just off Young Street West near Smithville, Ontario. My father was George Greves Patterson and my mother's name was Mary. Being the first born, I became the proud owner of several names. I was christened **Alan Kenneth McCulloch Patterson**, which was rather a nuisance when I had to sign my name in full.

Many years later ...

It wasn't until 1935 that I learned that the Canadian Marconi Company was running a school in Toronto to coach students for the Department of Transport Certificate in Radiotelegraphy. This was to obtain operators for their ships.

The autumn of 1935 found me rooming in Toronto and studying at the Marconi school on King Street. There were about 35 students in the class. It was a tough course (and it still is today) and only about five of us tried the exams in the spring. I tried my exams at the Department of Transport office in the spring of 1936 and was successful in obtaining my Second Class Certificate in Radiotelegraphy.

The year 1936 was still depression period and I waited all summer hoping for a call up to work. Fortunately, it came about the last of September and I was instructed to go to Sarnia and join the S/S Harmonic, a Canadian Steamship vessel that plied the Great Lakes and carried passengers and freight during the summer. At this time of the year it only carries package freight. We ran from Sarnia to Port Arthur (now Thunder Bay) until the thickening ice forced us to lay up at Sarnia. My old teacher suggested that

I should obtain my First Class Certificate in Radio-telegraphy in order to assure myself work next year.

January 1937 found me boarding once more in Toronto and back at the Marconi School. I found that I was the only one studying for a First Class Certificate. The subjects were harder and the code speed required was much greater, but in the spring of 1937 I tried my exams at the D.D. T. office and once more was successful. *I now was the proud owner of the Canadian First Class Certificate of Proficiency in Radio and my Certificate number was 3781, dated November 22nd, 1938.* I didn't have to wait so long for a ship this time; with my First Class ticket I "bumped" a Second Class operator on the S/S. Collier, another Canadian Steamship line vessel plying the lower lakes and carrying coal as the name implies.

The Next Year …

It was winter in Canada the 9th of January, 1938, and I was on my way to New York to join a British ship. Memories of the past few depression years passed through my mind: the struggle to find the necessary dollars for a technical education; the lines of unemployed waiting for their parcels of food and clothing; the families that had lost all their possessions through no fault of their own; the hard struggle for survival for so many people. For many people they had been hopeless and wasted years; the young could not afford to marry; the old could hardly afford to live. These were years etched deeply into the memories of many people.

I listened to the familiar and mournful howl of the T.H. @ B. whistle as we rushed through the Niagara countryside of Smithville, St. Anns and Welland. When would I see this Canadian country scene again, I wondered, as the train thundered on its way towards the United States.

I was on my way to join the British Marconi company and deep sea vessels. The wages would be lower than on Canadian ships but at least it would be year round employment and a chance to see the world and the people that inhabited it. This was the opportunity that I had been looking for.

Part 1
Early years in the British Merchant Marine

o o o o o o o o o o o o o o o o o o o o o o o o o o o o o o o o o o o o o o

'Tis all a Chequer-board of
Nights and Days
Where Destiny with Men
for pieces plays:
Hither and thither moves,
and mates, and slays,
And one by one back in the
Closet lays.

(Rubaiyat of Omar Khayyam)

Jan.9, 1938.

I am on my way to New York by train from Hamilton, Ontario, where I expect to join the British Wireless Marine Service as a Radio Officer. Everything has been arranged by the Canadian Marconi Company and there is a ship waiting for me. It's great to think of seeing far lands and strange new places—for all that though it was dashed hard to say good-bye at home. It may be years before I can get back and I suppose we will all be greatly changed by then. I'm wondering what New York will look like. It's no use trying to sleep tonight as my thoughts seem to keep time to the clicking of the wheels on the rails as we plunge through the darkness. I wonder if there will be a war before I see home again.

Jan. 10, 1938 (New York City)

It was early morning when I arrived at the huge Central Station on 42nd street and after having a shave and a haircut I took a taxi up to Beaver Street and the B.W.M.S. office. There I was assigned to the **S.S. Bellepline**, she is one of a bunch of ships that have been bought by the British from the Americans. They have been laid up for several years and are now being put into condition to cross the Atlantic. They are to be loaded up with scrap metal and when they reach Britain the ship and cargoes will both be scrapped. The Wireless Engineer brought me over to the ship, showed me the wireless gear and introduced me to the other officers. Another Canadian who had joined the Company was just shifted from here the other day to the **S.S. Mitchell.** The Captain slipped on some ice yesterday and is in hospital so I have not met him. The Chief Officer Mr. Soutar is a very genial sort, in fact they all are and they make me feel very much at home. After dinner several of us were chatting with the Steward who appears to be a man of parts. According to his story he was in the army for a number of years and was a member of the body-guard for Sir Malcolm Haily in India. After leaving that he claims to have tried his hand at forty-nine jobs in two years—surely almost a record. "Once", he said, "I applied for a job as a librarian when I was getting pretty hungry and desperate, there was a large crowd of applicants so I walked up to them as if I owned the place, told them that I was sorry but the vacancy had already been filled and offered to take their employment cards for future reference if they wanted to leave them. The bluff worked and they all walked away leaving me as the only applicant for the job and I landed it."

We are on the Brooklyn side of the river and will be helping the engineer install and repair wireless gear on several other ships for the next few days.

Jan. 13/38.

I have been suddenly transferred to the **S.S. Mitchell** as they found that the Government Inspector was not going to let them sail unless they either installed an auto-alarm or put on another Radio Officer. Here I met the chap who had been on the **Bellepline** for a while. It was about 1:30 PM when I was told to transfer and the ship was to sail at 4PM. On my arrival, after a mad scramble with taxis, signing on at the shipping office and catching a launch out to where the ship was anchored, I found that we were not sailing until morning. They had not been expecting me on board and had no cabin prepared for me. I expect that if I knew the ropes a bit better I would have plenty of reason to object. Still things will probably get straightened out before long. We are sailing for Portland, Maine, to pick up part of a cargo of scrap iron. The other "sparks" is a man of about forty-eight, although he has been in the radio game since it started he appears to know little more than I do about the antique radio gear that we have on this ship. The main transmitter is useless owing to the motor-generator being "frozen" solid with rust. Our only transmitter is a small lifeboat set. The receiver is one of the first battery sets put out and as uncertain as a mule. As this ship has been laid up for nine years and we will be crossing the North Atlantic in the winter time I'm rather wondering if it isn't a case of "fools walking where angels fear to tread."

Jan. 16/38 We are nearing Portland and have been having a lot of trouble with the telemeter steering gear and have made several stops to adjust it. We hope they get it set right before we try crossing the Atlantic. Tonight I listened to my first distress traffic on the air. The shore station **WMR** first sent out the auto-alarm signal then the information that station **SVQY**, the *SS. Aspasssia* was taking water through her bunkers: position approximately Lat. 35 Long 50.00W. Ships in the vicinity were asked to communicate with her. She was too far away for us to be of any use.

Jan. 18, 1938 (*The feel of the deck under their feet again*)

The crowd on here are mostly Scottish and were brought over from the U.K. to take the ship back. The other officers are all pretty old, most of them having been retired, but owing to the shortage of seamen in Britain they took the opportunity to make a bit of extra cash, and possibly to satisfy a longing to feel the deck under their feet once again. The crew look and act like a bunch of Glasgow toughs. I hear that most of them have bad discharges and according to the 3rd they would never be employed if there was not a shortage of seamen. My fellow Canadian seems to spend most of his time drinking and I'm afraid that I do not take to him much. I expect that is why he is still not in the radio branch of the Canadian civil services.

Jan. 22/38

Portland, Maine:

The weather is bitterly cold here but still I have been getting out enough to look the place over. It is a very old fashioned city set amid ideal surroundings. This morning it was sunny though cold and I walked out to the Eastern Promenade for a look around. It is on a hill overlooking the bay and there was a fine view. The silence was occasionally broken by a small fishing craft chugging into port or a flock of ducks whirring past overhead. Leaving there I inquired the way to the other end of the town. The gentleman that I asked immediately invited me to hop in his car and he said he would show me around as he had an hour to fill in. He was as good as his word and I certainly enjoyed the drive and the company. The Portland people are very proud of their city and enjoy showing it off to the visitors. The other Radio Officer Mr. P—has been wandering about in a drunken haze most of the time, making a nuisance of himself generally as well as making himself very unpopular with everybody. The crew have been living up to expectations. They act like wild Indians when they are drunk and it has been found necessary to keep a policeman on board both day and night. The police are very decent chaps and it is a relief to have them to talk to for a change. The Steward, 3rd and 4th Engineers are very decent chaps. The Steward is English but has been in the states for some years and is taking this way of getting back to see his mother. The 3rd Engineer had a good job ashore but had a longing to go back to sea for a trip so here he is, the job is waiting for him when he goes back to Glasgow. The 4th was a good sort and the only mistake he made was in drinking about a quart of the real hard "likker" that they brew around these parts. After that he promptly went up to the Captain's quarters and picked a fight with the "old man". The "old man" is quite a soak himself so he apparently held no grudge.

Jan. 28/38: Brooklyn, New York

Today I paid a visit to **"Radio City"** and found it very interesting. We went on what they call a "behind the scenes tour" where we saw how broadcasting was carried out at the studio. From behind soundproof glass partitions we watched orchestras, etc. playing and as we could hear no sound it looked most amusing. The guide showed us that those studios were actually floating on felt. We had a brief glimpse at the many control panels and the guide said that electric power was supplied from eight different sources so that if one failed there was always another source of supply. From a sound-proof studio through an amplifier he demonstrated how sound effects were produced over the 4 way radio. A bunch of wooden pegs set in a frame were pounded up and down and along with the orders given at the same time sounded exactly like a company of soldiers marching. Cellophane squeezed in the hand sounded like the crackling of flames, etc.

Leaving "*Radio City*" I wandered on up to 8th Avenue, past Columbus Circle and at length came to Central Park where many people were enjoying the fine sunny weather. Going on a bit farther I came to the American Museum of Natural Arts. I entered the huge planetarium that is connected with the museum and it is certainly worth a visit. It has a vast stainless steel dome with the horizon of New York painted around the edge. As the lights were gradually dimmed it gave the impression that one was out in the open. A complicated looking magic lantern studded with many arms threw the natural-looking reproduction of the heavens on the darkened dome above us. By merely pressing buttons the lecturer showed us what the stars looked like a year ago. Then he showed us how each star would be placed tonight and how they would look in another year. He showed us how they looked in the early evening, how they had and would look at various times of the night and then they gradually faded into the dawn in a most natural manner. Truly it is a wonderful machine and it is certainly worth a visit.

It was evening as I strolled back past the Columbus Circle and up Broadway. Thousands of brilliantly lighted signs were flashing up the "*Great white way*" and hundreds of people were scurrying about as if their time was worth a lot of money. Near Times Square I stopped at a restaurant and had a good lunch. Already I am appreciating a change from ship's fare.

Feb. 4, 1938 (*Good-bye New York*)

I said good-bye to New York in the early evening. Our anchor-chain rattled up into the chain locker, the telegraph bells tinkled and the little tugs fussily pushed and pulled us out into the stream. Slowly we nosed our way out past the Statue of Liberty, a dazzling figure outlined against the evening sky, and on past the huge skyscrapers with their millions of twinkling lights. Slowly they faded into the distance until they became a mere glow and I confess that I felt a bit melancholy as I reflected that I might not see any more of America for a long, long time.

P—is just recovering from a prolonged bout with the bottle and tonight when he came to relieve me he looked so haggard and sick that I felt rather sorry for him and offered to take over his watch. He had assured me that he had no more whiskey. I also took over a couple of his four hour watches between Portland and New York when he was too drunk to relieve me and I must say it is becoming a bit tiresome especially as he hasn't enough good breeding to thank a person for it.

Feb. 9, 1938 (*North Atlantic Ocean*)

We are ploughing through a rising gale and the waves tower above us like mountains at times. Heavily laden as we are the waves often sweep down over the decks, tons of swirling green water that would sweep you overboard in no time if it caught you unaware. Last night just after I had come off watch and was turning in a great wave swept right over the boat deck, the ship keeled way over and hung there for a short while, then she slowly began to right herself but only got half way up when another huge wave hit her and she repeated the performance. Fortunately she managed to slowly right herself that time. The alleyways were flooded with water and the cabins at the end had several feet of water splashing about in them. Fortunately mine is well forward and so escaped the water. This morning I found *that many thought the ship was going to turn over but "ignorance is bliss" and I had thought it merely the usual Atlantic style of doing things.*

Feb. 10, 1938 (*A night I will never forget*)

North Atlantic Ocean—Last night was a night that I don't think I will ever forget. I was doing the midnight watch and listening to the gale raging outside above the hum of my headphones when suddenly the door flung open and P—staggered into the room. He was trembling like a leaf and looked to be in a horrible state. He started raving about the 3rd mate and I making noises outside his cabin and declared that he could hear me sending out code to him. As he was out of whiskey and had not been drinking I could not make out what was wrong with him at first. When he suddenly made a dive for the receiving gear and tried to pull the earphones off to stop the code that he claimed he was hearing, I dragged him out of the wireless cabin and partly carried him to his cabin. He was suffering from the famous D.T.'s as a result of too much drink in port and a sudden stoppage of it at sea. I put him to bed and gave him some hot tea and aspirins and then went up on watch again.

About half an hour later the door flew open once more and there was our wild-eyed friend staring at me again. I have no craving for the dramatic and suddenly the thought of being cooped up in a lonely radio cabin with a man like that in the middle of the stormy North Atlantic didn't appeal to me at all. I found myself heartily wishing that I was reading about it in some book or other. Cold shivers insisted on running up and down my spine.

I kept between him and the wireless gear that time and I watched him pretty closely to make sure he didn't lay his hands on anything that might prove dangerous should he take the notion. Gradually he calmed down and I think that I almost convinced him that it was all just a bad dream.

With the help of the Bosun he was half carried and half dragged off to bed once more.

While the Bosun watched him I tried to wake up the "old man" but he just wouldn't waken. We had thought we might get some sleeping drug out of the medicine chest and give it to P—. Anyway I had to go back on watch so told the Bos'un to watch him until he went to sleep before he went on with his other duties and then slip up on the bridge for a minute and told the 2nd officer what had happened.

Just before dawn P—came tumbling into the wireless room once again but he did not appear to be nearly so bad and was apparently seeing fewer pink elephants, etc. He soon quieted down and I called for the Bosun who helped me get P—back to his room again. After going off watch I looked into his cabin and he seemed much better. By breakfast time he seemed quite normal again but I took over his watch. One of the other officers suggested that a good dose of Epsom salts might do him a lot of good so the advice was acted upon. Later on he appeared well enough that the Captain allowed him to resume his normal watch so I went and turned in. About an hour later I was awakened by P—! The "old man", 2nd and 3rd mates are in the "old man's cabin," he said, "and they are talking of demoting me to cabin boy. You go and see what you can do for me will you?" Of course I realized right away what was wrong so assured P.—that I would be right up. On going up to the bridge I found P.—hanging around the Captain's door with an anxious expression on his face and nothing would do but that I would go right in and see the "old man". I knocked and went in and as I expected there was the "old man" quietly reading a magazine. I told him that P—had the D.T.'s again and he told me to take charge of the radio room until P—was better and to see that he was kept away from the instruments. On going into the Radio room I looked to see what kind of a log P—had been keeping and found the following note written in P-'s neat handwriting: "Am being demoted to the rank of cabin boy by the Captain because for some unknown reason I went out of my mind last night but am OK now after a thorough cleaning out with Epsom salts".

He became worse during the day and complained of having pains in his head, also he kept imagining that we were wanting to throw him overboard. I talked the "Old Man" into ordering a man to stand watch over him so that he would do no harm to himself or to someone else and by ten PM he was a handful even for the husky sailor who was watching him. He kept trying to escape and kept imagining all sorts of things until at length they drugged him to sleep at about 1AM.

Feb.11/38 (North Atlantic Ocean)

To everyone's relief P—was quite normal once again when he woke up. He has resumed his regular watches once more and we hope that he will have no more trouble for the rest of the trip. The gale has slackened off and perhaps we may get a bit of good weather now.

Feb.19/38-(Off Land's End)

A beautiful star-lit night with the lights of *Land's End* sparkling in the distance and the sweet smell of land and peat smoke in the air. We have had wonderful weather for the past few days. As it will still be dark when we pass through *The Straits of Dover* tomorrow night I guess I won't get to see them.

Feb. 22/38—Scotland

Tall and rather grim looking hills were my first glimpse of Scotland. Shrouded in a winter's haze and without a tree on them that I could see, and only the lone farm building here and there. It made me rather wonder if the rest of Scotland was so hard and barren looking—but of course it can't be.

Feb. 23/38 ... Glasgow, Scotland.

This morning we sailed up under the famous Firth of Forth bridge and docked at Rosyth where the ship and cargo will both be scrapped and used to build better ships. We had a fine bus ride over the winding road to Glasgow. The quaint little villages that we passed through quite delighted me. Many of the houses had thatched roofs and others had roofs of red tile. The road seemed to wind right between the houses in places and I suppose most of them had been there for longer than I care to look back.

Feb. 25th/38 (Glasgow, Scotland)

We reported at the B.W.M.S. depot yesterday and we were officially signed up with the company as from January 10th. Tonight P—left to join an Australian bound ship at Newcastle. I was dashed glad to see the last of him and though he shed a few beery tears on saying good-bye to me I certainly felt no sorrow of any kind. Of course he neglected to thank me for all the extra watches I had kept for him. They tell me at the depot that I may have to wait a few days for a ship but as I am on full shore allowance why I should worry. It will give me a good chance to look around a bit and to buy my uniforms, etc.

Feb. 27/38 (Glasgow, Scotland)

Today I strolled down along the Clyde. Standing at Stobcross Quay I looked at the many ships that were busy discharging cargo. Large Clyde dray-horses pulled their heavily laden wagons over the cobblestone streets as they passed between the ships and the warehouses. Several Lascar sailors from an Indian-run ship passed me, chattering among themselves in a strange tongue as they went. The air was fragrant with the smell of spice and molasses. All along the Clyde huge cranes loomed up against the horizon and along the river one can hear the riveters at work and the clatter of steel plates. There is a saying that *"Glasgow made the Clyde and the Clyde made Glasgow"*. When you reflect upon the fact that the Clyde was once merely a shallow stream and has been dredged out to its present size, and that the ship-building trade along its banks is the main lively-hood of the greater part of Glasgow's populations, it is quite easily seen that one cannot do without the other. Not so long ago the ship yards were idle and it seemed that the depression would never end but today every yard is busy and Glasgow is prospering once more. The Clyde is again sending forth fine ships to sail the seven seas and her sons are sent forth as fine engineers.

The huge black tenement houses that spread forth through the city are pretty grim looking things. The only thing that relieves their monotonous appearance is that when you look down over them from a hill top (and there are a lot of hills in Glasgow) the chimney-pots make a rather picturesque scene.

Feb. 28th/38 (Glasgow, Scotland)

The sun chased away the early morning mists as I strolled up to St. Enoch's station where St. Enoch's Church formerly stood. I was heading for St. George's Square when I was lured from my path by the beautiful sound of pealing bells. At length I found where the bells were hung. They were in the old steeple at Glasgow Cross that used to be a part of Tolbooth Debtor's prison. Here prisoners used to lower their shoes by means of string to collect coins from sympathetic passer-byes below. The large wooden door is studded with irons, the steeple itself is about one hundred and thirteen feet high and contains forty eight bells. The place was made famous by Sir Walter Scott who mentioned it in his *"Rob Roy"*.

South from the Cross runs the old Saltmarket Street where the rich merchants used to have their offices times long past. Today it has been mostly torn down to do away with the slums that had taken the place of rich merchants and the clinking of golden coins. To the west of the Cross on the south side of the road is the old Tron Steeple, all that remains after a disastrous fire.

Turning north I went up High Street to Glasgow Cathedral. As I stood admiring it the bells began to ring. Deciding that it would be a fine idea to go to the services in the Cathedral, I hid my camera under my rain coat, draped the coat over my arm and walked in with rather a few misgivings. The vast nave seems a very impressive place when you enter it. There are many huge stone columns supporting the roof and all around the sides and on the floor are the nameplates of those who are buried within. I followed the others into the Lower Church and sat down in a very narrow and hard phew.

The service was different from anything I had ever seen before. I enjoyed it immensely. The early morning sun streaming through the beautiful stained glass windows; the massive stone columns; the knowledge that God had been worshiped at that spot for over 1500 years and the chanting of the choir left me with a memory that I would treasure for many years. The Upper Church is a huge building in itself. Some idea of its size may be demonstrated by the fact that there are one hundred and fifty great stone pillars supporting its roof. The cathedral is built along simple yet beautiful Gothic lines that seem to make it look even larger than it really is.

After the service I strolled down what is known as Bell O" the Brae and so back to the Cross where I caught a tram and went out to Linn Park. Linn Park is a beautiful place with many rolling acres. Although only the last of February it is spring here. The grass lawns are green and the spring birds were singing. I came upon an old ruined castle in one corner of the park and started chatting to one of the keepers, who, it turned out had been in Canada for several years. Although the castle was not open to the public he offered to show me through it. There was not really much to see except the great thick walls and the ruined dungeon. It was close to the castle where Mary Queen of Scots had watched the battle of Langside.

Leaving Linn Park I took a tram across the city to Kelvingrove Park. This park is close to the impressive looking Glasgow University. By the time I had finished strolling about it was getting late in the evening and time to return to lodgings.

March 3rd/38 (Glasgow, Scotland)

During the day I have to stay around the British Wireless Merchant Service Depot but after about four pm. I am free to wander. I have been rather amused by the variety of shops along the main streets. Butcher shops with sheep hanging up, their noses rubbing the blood-stained sawdust below, expensive dress shops, fruit shops and jewelery shops all stand side by side along with every other kind of shop.

No one seems to take the threat of war very seriously here. In Canada it seemed to be the chief topic of conversation but here football seems to be the all prevailing subject. Either we Canadians must take life too seriously or else these people are getting used to living alongside a volcano. Everyone seems so friendly here that it is a real treat after New York where everyone is far too busy to be friendly. If you ask the direction to any place as you go along the street they often walk part way there with you to show you the way. It seems to rain most of the time in this portion of the world but no one appears to take any notice of it. If you mention it they appear a bit surprised, as though wondering what else anyone would expect it to do. I am having a bit of trouble understanding the broad Glasgow-Scotch tongue, it's as though they were talking with a hot potato in their mouths but I am beginning to understand it a bit better as time goes on.

March 7/38 (Glasgow, Scotland)

I had a glorious week-end. I met a gentleman on the tram to Edinburgh city and when he found that I was a Canadian he offered to show me around. He was a law student and well versed in the history of Edinburgh. We crossed the Princess Garden bridge and climbed up the Castle Hill. I wandered up and down the Royal Mile with my new found friend pointing out the points of interest. His voice fairly glowed with pride at times as he spoke of the days of Scotland's glory. I felt proud to think that my ancestors were Scotch as well. After looking over the hill as best one can at night we descended to the city and had tea. Unfortunately he had an important engagement for the night so we were not able to meet again but he gave me his address and a real hearty invitation to look him up the next time I was here. I certainly appreciated his showing me around like that and do hope to meet him again sometime.

Early Sunday morning I left the hotel where I was staying and set out to see the sights by the light of day. First I climbed up Carlton Hill from where I could look down over the city. Black smoke was ascending from the thousands of picturesque looking chimney-pots below ... lums the

Scotch call them.... and at time it rather obscured the view. Once in a while the haze would lift and I could see the silvery waters of the *Firth of Forth* in the distance. Not so far away I could see the Braid Hills while closer at hand was the *Castle hill* with Edinburgh castle outlined against its summit. I asked a gentleman what the twelve giant stone columns standing along the top of Carlton Hill had been. "That", he answered, "is called *Edinburgh Humiliation* by some people. It was started as a National memorial in commemoration of the battle of Waterloo and was to be a copy of the Parthenon at Athens, but it was never completed owing to lack of funds"

On another corner of the hill stands *Nelson's monument* built to look like a spy glass (telescope). As I stood looking down over the city the church bells began to ring, their tones mellowed by the distance and rising and falling in their throbbing summons to Divine worship.

An hour later I was on the Castle Hill and walking along Lawn-market Street which is part of the Royal Mile, the road that connects Hollyrood Palace with Edinburgh Castle. I talked to a very distinguished looking gentleman who gave me some interesting information. Later on he informed me that he was a guide to touring parties during the summer tourist season. I was so attracted by his rolling R's and distinguished manner that I hired him on the spot to escort me around the hill for the rest of the afternoon and show me the points of interest in detail. He led me through many mysterious looking alleyways into courtyards that were fairly packed with history. He showed me the brass plate that marks the last resting place of John Knox and later on we passed by the Heart of Medlothian that is outlined in the bricks of the pavement. Then we came to the house where John Knox is said to have lived: It was a very attractive looking old place with balconies jutting out over the street. One old house that we passed had a carved effigy of a turbaned Moore above the first floor. The story is told of a local boy who had to flee the city in olden days owing to some misdemeanor and so he fled to Morocco. He became a rich man there and at length he returned to Edinburgh. His misdeeds were forgiven

him and he married into a good family and built the house with the turbaned Moore upon it.

Holy Rood Palace, of course, is steeped in history. This was the home of
the Kings and Queens of Scotland since the sixteenth century. This was
also home to Mary Queen of Scots where she lived a troubled and passion-
ate life. My guide pointed out the spot where Rizzio, her reputed lover, lay
after he was murdered and the stairway that they had crept up to carry out
their grim mission. It took no great stretch of imagination to imagine the
unhappy Queen Mary in this great palace or to recall the days of glory that
it had seen.

Returning up the Royal Mile we passed the kilted sentries and entered the
castle grounds. Words can hardly describe the impression that the great,
grim looking castle makes upon one. What a story it could tell—of
armored knights, of battles fought, of pomp and pageantry, of victory and
defeat; of everything that goes to make up the history of an ancient nation.

My guide took me to the Scottish National War Memorial that is inside
the castle walls. It is the most beautiful memorial that I have seen both
outside and inside. The guide explained the significance of each bit of
carving as we first walked around the outside and then entered within. The
center shrine is built on natural rock and encloses the roll of honor—those
who died for king and country during the Great War. Overhanging the
shrine is the figure of St. Michael "*Captain of the Heavenly Hosts.*" I parted
with my guide outside the castle; he the richer; I, the wiser. It was surely a
most profitable exchange for both of us.

It was evening as I strolled through Princess Gardens along the foot of
Castle Hill. The melodious chimes of St. Cuthberts began to send their
mellow notes into the evening air, rising and falling in unison and making
one want to just stand and listen to the beauty of their pealing. Above me
the Castle Hill and the grim old castle stood outlined against the horizon.
The serrated battlements of the castle made one expect to hear the call of a

bugle and to see armored knights looking down at one. They looked like silent guardians over the great city below. Only darkness and the necessity of catching my bus drove me away from my meditations at the foot of Castle Hill and surely it would be well worth a trip back there at any time.

March 10/38 … (Glasgow, Scotland)

I signed on the *S/S Marslew* today, she is a 4540 ton ship bound for Liverpool, Cape Verde Islands and South America. Will be leaving here in a few days.

March 16th/38—Liverpool, England.

We reached here the day before yesterday after a rough passage from Glasgow. The docks are very busy and one hears the clatter of horses feet and the rattle of drays all day long over the cobbled streets as they cart the merchandise away to the warehouses. Steam lorries also seem to be very popular. They are the first I have ever seen and I find them rather interesting. I had thought they were out of date years ago. The streets in this city seem to run in any old direction and I invariably get lost when I wander forth. This is definitely a sailor's town and everything seems to be about ships and shipping.

March 17th/38: Liverpool, England.

Today I took a ferry over the Mersey to Birhenhead and there caught a bus to the old world city of Chester. Stepping out of the bus it seemed as if I had stepped out of a stage-coach into the 16th or 17th century. It had a sort of *"Pickwick Papers"* atmosphere and I could just imagine Charles Dickens walking around these streets making mental notes. The town is surrounded by a complete wall and the houses have the original "olde English" wood and plaster fronts with bay windows and ornate woodwork. Another feature of the place are the "rows". They consist of two storied buildings and along the front of the second story there runs a wide stone sidewalk. As you walk along you can watch the pedestrians and motor traffic below or else gaze into the shop windows. Their presence is explained by the fact that in olden days the roadway used to be knee-deep in mud in the rainy weather so the "rows" were built for the convenience of the shoppers. It was a perfect spring day so I walked around the old stone wall and from its top (it has a wide path-way along it) I had some fine views down over the surrounding countryside. Standing at one corner of the wall is the *King Charles Tower* where King Charles watched the battle of Rowton Moor and the defeat of his forces on Sept. 24th, 1645.

On one side the wall follows along the canal and some say that at one time it was a moat. Still walking along the wall I came to the North Gate which in the olden days contained the city jail and the dungeon known as "*Little Ease*". A little further on I passed the watch tower known as *Morgan's Mount*. The cathedral must surely be one of the finest in existence. It was originally a Benedictine monastery and one can well imagine the days when it was a sanctuary for those who fell foul of the law. I wondered if our generation would be able to produce anything so fine for future generations to gaze upon. It is of course impossible for anyone to see all of Chester in part of a day; I would very much like to go back some day and spend several days there just wandering around seeing those old and interesting sights.

March 19th/38

This evening we slipped down the River Mersey on the tide and so to sea. Now we will be several weeks at sea.

March 28th/38: St. Vincent, Cape Verde Islands off the African coast.

Arrived here this morning and we are anchored out in the bay unloading into lighters. This is the most desolate place I have ever seen and there is nothing to go ashore to see. The island is mostly sand and even the palm trees look stunted and discouraged. The red tile roofed cottages are nestled at the foot of a hot looking sand hill. There are only two or three white men here amid the several thousand starved looking Negroes. The Negroes paddle out in small canoes and try to exchange the half wild fruit they have gathered from another island for any kind of clothing; they have little use for money here and ask enormous prices for anything because they have so little use for it and they would rather have old clothing in exchange.

One of the white men here had asked the Captain to bring him a bowler hat from England and tonight he came on board to get it. He threw the old one away and put the new one on so as to avoid paying customs duty. Just as he was walking along the deck to depart a violent gust of wind sent the hat flying into the sea and in the darkness there was no recovering it. Tough luck because he will be unable to get another one for several months and he threw his old bowler away. For an old shirt I received several dozen oranges and bananas and several coco-nuts; they will be a welcome addition to the fare during the next few weeks at sea.

April 3rd/38: At sea.

We crossed the equator this morning and it was my first time across. There was not even a bump as we went over it! My shipmates seem to be a very good bunch. The *"old man"* is quite a young Irishman and I rather like him. The mate comes from the Shetlands and talks with the sort of whine peculiar to the Islanders. The second mate is a slow speaking Londoner and the 3rd mate is a dark and rather gloomy young man from Devon. The chief Engineer is a middle aged, rotund man with a good sense of humor who hails from Bridlington, England. The second Engineer might prove to be Welsh and he is usually grumbling while the third is a Swed who would be offended if you called him other than English. The 4th informs me that he hails from "artlepool." The food on this ship is just so-so, and the cockroaches are terrible. We have a couple of passengers, an elderly Englishman and his wife who are returning to the Argentine after a visit to England. He is retired but his pension is not sufficient to keep them in England. He is the finicky, semi-livery type but his wife is charming.

April 16/38 … Montevidio, Uruguay

The place is a bit on the shabby side and not at all like the tropical paradise that I was expecting. Some of the plazas are rather nice though and I have now walked under my first palm trees in the tropics. Everyone speaks Spanish so it is hard to find your way around. Owing to a certain clause in our contract I have to relieve the officer checking cargo if required or if necessary check the cargo. Only the skin-flint companies take advantage of it but this is one of them. I have only had to relieve the 2nd mate at meal-time so far though. It is rather fun watching the Spanish stevedores. We are unloading whiskey and they slam the cases down hard so as to try to break the bottles. When a bottle breaks one of them holds it up in the air and the others crowd around and cup their hands under it and get a free drink. We are leaving here tonight and it is about eighteen hours up the muddy Plate river to Buenos Aires

April 20th/38—Buenos Aires, Argentina

I have been here several days now with lots of time to look around. This is indeed a fine city but it is just a bit too much like New York for my liking. Except for the fact that the people speak Spanish one might mistake the buildings for a city in North America. The city is built on a level plain, the plazas are beautiful and well kept and the people dress as we do in North America. It is winter here now with fairly cool nights and fairly hot days. At one time this city had the reputation of being one of the wickedest cities in the world but all that is now a thing of the past and today it jealously guards it's good reputation.

The first evening in port Mr. Newbury the 3rd mate and I headed for what is known as the *"Farmyard bar"* where we did away with a large and well cooked meal. This meal included nice juicy steaks to which we had pledged ourselves before when well out to sea. The *"Farmyard Bar"* is built to resemble a large barn: it has a fine orchestra and dance floor and in front of the orchestra hangs a sign that says in three languages, *"Anyone caught wringing the bell must stand the orchestra a drin*k". Underneath it hangs a very convenient cow bell. Most things here seem to be built with the Latin eye for beauty. It has been said of Buenos Aires that *"it is as modern as New York, as beautiful as any Spanish city and as gay as Paris."* I also find the quaint sidewalk cafes a good place to people watch.

Sad to say some of these Argentines are inclined to be a bit tricky. The other day I went into a barber shop for a haircut—usual cost about 90 centimes. The tall, dopey looking barber that cut my hair ran some sort of machine over it, then before I knew it had started shampooing my hair. I began to ask what the big idea was but he pretended not to understand and tipped the chair back and started to give me a facial massage. Feeling much like a drowning man and with visions of an enormous bill I started to protest most vigorously and most reluctantly he let me up out of the chair. He wrote the bill out and it was about five pesos more than it should have been. I was so angry that I omitted to give him the usual ten percent tip. Today the chief Engineer was telling us about someone who had a large bill run up in a barber shop and was saying that it was a common thing here. I didn't say that I knew all about it having had it happen to me as I knew I would never hear the last of it on board. Anyway it is useless to raise much of a fuss about things like that when you cannot speak the language. A foreigner is bound to come off the worse in almost any country. They have a fine big post office here and every time I have been there I have been short changed; and that I hear is usual.

April 24th/38—Buenos Aires

Today the Chief Engineer and I decided to go to the races so we caught a train out to Belgrano. On reaching the track we found no one there and realized that we had gone to the wrong track. The other track was at the other side of the city so we decided it was not worth going to it and began to wonder what we could do to pass away the afternoon. We saw several groups of people going somewhere so we decided to follow them. On reaching a gateway we paid a Peso each and were handed programs printed in Spanish which we could not understand. We found that we had stumbled upon an army cavalry versus civilian field-day. The horses all looked splendid and there were some exciting jumps and spills and everyone was enjoying it all. There were some lovely looking senoritas and I found myself wishing that I could speak Spanish. The show was rather spoiled at the end by a downpour of rain. Later on we boarded a train at Belgrano again and returned to the Retiro station and the city.

Tonight I had my first ride in one of the "colectivos"-my first and I hope, my last one. The colectivo's idea was started by a taxi driver several years ago during the height of the depression. His idea was to make a nominal charge of ten centimes for each passenger and to run the taxi along the same route regularly. The idea caught on and all sorts of top-heavy and decrepit affairs are used today. The drivers drive with true Latin disregard for life and limb and are often involved in accidents. Our ride was breath-taking to say the least and we were thankful to set foot on solid ground again.

May 1st/38—Buenos Aires

The Mate, Chief Engineer, 3rd mate and I all went to the races at Palmero this afternoon. We went out by bus and train as today was Labor-Day. There was not a taxi to be found and as a result we were late getting there. We didn't quite know how to place our bets or how much the tickets cost but I shoved five Pesos through the wicket the first time and named the horse and out came three Pesos change with the ticket. Just as the Mate was going to follow my example the wicket was slammed down so I sold him half of my ticket and we strolled over to the grandstand just in time to see our horse romp home last. My next bet was a winner and I made over eleven Pesos. We had a good afternoon and it was very interesting watching the crowds. The Chief Engineer is a keen photographer and he was taking a snap of the horses passing the winning post when the Mate slapped him on the back (he had not noticed him taking the snap) you should have heard what the Chief said! We ended the day by having dinner at Adam's bar and then for the sake of doing something different we hired a horse and garry and trundled down Florida Street which is reserved for pedestrians. The good Buenos Airians merely stared at the mad Englishmen and nothing was said about it.

May 2nd/38

Buenos Aires for the last few days we have been docked opposite one of the huge frigerificos (meat packing plants) The smell is overpowering and don't think I shall like tinned meat anymore. We are leaving for Villa Constitution tomorrow.

May 5th/38 (Villa Constitution, Argentina)

It was an interesting trip up the muddy and winding Parana river. The river banks were well wooded with here and there a lonely wood-cutters cabin. The river is so winding that often you may think another ship is behind you when you see it through the trees but it is actually ahead. Gradually the trees became thinner until we at last came out into lonely plain country with occasional herds of cattle grazing upon it. Then ranch houses became more numerous and at length we reached this lonely little village. Last night the Chief Engineer introduced me to an Anglo-Argentine family; the father was English. There were two lovely daughters who spoke fairly good English and several sturdy sons. They gave us the first "matte" to drink that I had tasted. It is a drink much favored by the native "gauchos" (cowboys) and is served in a matte cup that is passed around and everyone drinks from the same cup. It is made the same as tea out of a sort of dry green leaf and sugar is sometimes added. As each person drinks up his share of matte more hot water is added to it and the next person has a go at it. I was the only one present who had not tasted it and all eyes were upon me as I took the first drink. I managed to bear up bravely and told them I liked it. We had a very pleasant evening there and tomorrow Mr. Gold (The Chief's friend) is taking us out to a vineyard to buy wine for the saloon table on the homeward journey.

May 6th/38(A death)

Our trip to the vineyards had to be postponed today as this morning the Bosun was found dead at the foot of the steep cliff that runs along the river here where we are docked. His companions say that he had indulged in quite a few glasses of local canya (the drink that makes you drunk for several days after) when he left them and apparently he missed the regular path on his way back and down the cliff he tumbled. His funeral was this afternoon and as is usual a representative was there from every other ship in port. The hearse was drawn by two horses along the clay roads and the cemetery was well out in the country. It was a Catholic cemetery and very decorative. It seemed a bit hard that a man should have to be buried so far from his native land and friend but I don't suppose it really matters though. I suppose that nearly every corner of this globe contains the remains of at least one British sailor. Diseases, fevers and accidents all take their toll of course in many a foreign port.

May 8th/38: Villa Constitution, Argentina

Today we made our postponed trip out to the vineyard where we met the owner, Signor Pacifico Cardanelly, an elderly man with a young wife and child. The Chief Engineer had been there before of course and we were made very welcome. Jugs of wine were drawn from the casks for us to sample and then we went out and had a look over the vineyard. I saw my first tangerines growing on the trees as well as grapefruit and lemons. On our return to the large rambling house we were pressed to help ourselves to all the wine we wanted and tea and cakes were also served. Then the Signor hitched up his horse to a high two wheeled cart and we piled the demijohns of wine and ourselves into it. The Chief picked up the reins whereupon the horse immediately started to back up and almost landed us in Signor Cardanelly's kitchen. The wheels of all the carts are made very high here owing to the deeply rutted clay roads during the rainy season.

May 13th/38: Rosario, Argentina

We arrived here several days ago and it did not take us long to get here as it is only an hours run up the river from Villa Constitution. This is a nice little city with well kept plazas, of course the plazas take first place in any Argentine town. Tonight the Chief Engineer took me to an interesting place called the Sefri Café. The Chief told me that several years ago there was a garri driver who patiently waited for passengers outside the cafes. One of his regular passengers was an old lady who in time died and left the garri driver her fortune. He built a block of buildings and the Sefri Care is in them. It is a beautiful spot and even well seasoned travelers declare that it is the nicest that they have seen. The high walls have beautiful wood carvings and the place is well lighted by hundreds of shapely chandeliers and the orchestra adds to the attraction of the place. We are loading wheat for the U.K. here and will soon be away again.

May 19th/38 Montevideo

It is morning and we have stopped here for a few hours to take on fuel and then will be away to sea for several weeks. So now it is good-bye to South America. It has been a great visit and I hope to come back again some day.

June 17th/38 S/S Marslew

At sea today the 4th Engineer indignantly showed me the remains of a new patrol jacket of his. As it was getting a bit soiled he put it in what looked like a nice clean tub of water. When he went back to take it out he found that only a few buttons were left as the water (so called) had turned out to be acid.

June 19th/38—Manchester Canal

Tonight we are sailing up the famous Manchester Canal. It looks great to see green grass and trees again after over thirty days at sea. I never knew they could look so good before. We passed under another canal tonight on our way up (believe it or not) it's a barge canal and the bridge swings back to let the big ships pass under it on their way up the Manchester canal.

June 20th/38—Manchester

We are tied up at the Saltford docks and have reported at my depot today. As the **Marslew** is going into dry-dock for survey I will not be sailing on her again.

June 21st/38.—Liverpool—England

Today I signed off the **Marslew** and came to Liverpool by train. I was sorry to have to say good-bye to my shipmates, particularly the Chief

Engineer, who had seemed to delight in showing me around. The jovial Irish Captain has certainly been a good sort as well and he was never above playing a game of chess or spinning a yarn. I do not suppose I shall ever meet them again as I am beginning to realize that this world is a lot bigger place than a lot of people think it is.

June 24th/38

Signed on the **S/S Contractor,** a Harrison Bros. ship today and we are sailing tomorrow for India. When I reach India I will be transferring to the Indian Coast for about two years. I have not had time to do much here but the necessary shopping in readiness for my coming isolation in the east. I have become quite friendly with a couple of chaps where I am staying as they are both sailors. I occasionally manage to get the red headed chap talking about the West African coast where he had been sailing for some time and it was worth listening to his stories about Africa. The other chap is studying for his mates ticket and was quite worried about it. Despite that he showed that he possessed a keen sense of humor and I enjoyed his company and his ready wit. Well we have said our good-byes tonight as have already sent my gear down to the ship and I must join her tomorrow morning.

June 25th/38

This evening the tugs pulled and shoved us out into the Mersey and we are now leaving the great city of Liverpool behind us. I wonder how long it will really be before I see those queer looking Liver Birds again as they perch on the top of the huge municipal buildings.

This ship is about 6,000 tons gross and I am looking forward to a very pleasant trip out to India on her. The crew are all Indian lascars on this ship except for the wheels men who are English. The saloon crowd are all Indians and I have an Indian *"boy"* to wait on me now. Fortunately for me he speaks English. I have a fine large cabin and a good wireless cabin; both of them are on the boat deck and so I have a very nice deck to myself.

June 29/38—Off Cape St. Vincent

The ship's dynamo has broken down and we will have to go into Gibraltar for a couple of days to get it repaired. This is certainly a very good ship with a fine crowd on her. Its quite nice to have an Indian *"boy"* to clean my shoes etc. and I am getting used to it. The food is slightly better on here than on the *Marslew* and we get morning and afternoon tea extra which is a decided advantage. The boy brings it up to my cabin. At the table the *"boys"* stand at ones elbow and seem to know just when you want the butter or the salt, etc. They tell me that on the coastal ships in India that there are even more *"boys"* to wait on one, particularly on the British India ships. Incidentally a native *"boy"* includes any Indian waiter who is between the ages of five to eighty years of age and my boy here is old enough to be my father yet they are always addressed as *"boy"*.

Of course the *"boys"* also take care of our laundry and cleaning our uniforms. Sometimes my clothes come back in not quite the same condition as when they left so instead of being angry at my *'boy'* I decided to write a poem.

I call my poem **"Ode to the Indian Dhobiewalla"!**

"You have torn my shorts and ripped my shirts,
Broken the buttons until it hurts;
You have marrowed my clothes with such right good will
I can hardly believe they are the same clothes still;
The higher the price that clothing goes
The broader your grin and the harder your blows
As you marrow my clothes on the dhobie rock
And mutter with glee "sahib's in for a shock".
(Written by A.K.M.P.)
*Marrow—to hit, strike.

My wireless gear on here is much more imposing than on the *Marslew* and includes an Auto Alarm, a machine that is supposed to register the auto-alarm signal that is sent out before an SOS and sets all sorts of bells ringing when it registers such a signal. I have to leave it in circuit when I am off watch.

June 30th/38

Today I experienced a thrill as we passed between the shores of Europe and Africa; then up past the towering rock of Gibraltar and so up into the spacious bay where we now lie at anchor waiting for the dynamo to be repaired. The hills of sunny Spain surround the bay and it seems hard to believe that civil war is now raging in that unhappy land. A small town nestles along the foot of Gibraltar and it looks as though it would be a rather desolate place to live. I do not expect to get ashore here as we are a long ways out in the bay and anyway my funds are running low.

In port the early morning sound was of chipping hammers as the native crew (known as lascars) made the plates ready for more paint. This is an endless job on any well run vessel. Decks were scrubbed and hosed down before breakfast and all was made ship-shape before the heat of the day. Every so often the Captain would do an inspection tour of the ship and woe betide the man who had not done his job properly.

July 4th/38

Here we are still at Gibraltar but expect to be leaving by tomorrow. I have been quite fascinated by the sight of several dozen lascars saying their prayers on the poop-deck in the evenings. *They usually stand in a double row* a*nd have a sort of cheer-leader who stands out in front. They always face Mecc*a as they pray. The weather is warm here but not too hot with a nice land breeze at night. We are having a rather pleasant time loafing around doing nothing and playing quoits and everyone including the Captain likes to play. There is also a dart board here that is much in use and I am becoming quite skilled in *Ye Olde English* game. This morning I was awake early and watched the sun rise over the rolling Spanish hills. Dozens of roosters were crowing their heads off as though to announce it's appearance and the smell of fresh mown hay in the air made me think of Ontario in the summertime.

July 9th/38

The weather is quite warm in the Mediterranean and the moonlit nights have been calm with splashes of phosphorescence along the sides of the ship. The water is an intense blue when seen by the light of the day and it feels great to be alive with such weather as we have been having. Yesterday we passed the Italian penal island of Pantallaria.

July 12th/38

This morning we reached Port Said at an early hour and were immediately besieged by a mob of be-fezzed and unscrupulous Egyptian rascals. There was no way to avoid them. They tried to sell us everything from dirty post-cards to wormy dates and they simply would not be chased. They had the habit of thrusting their goods into our cabins despite all vigorous protests and claiming that it was a gift. In about five minutes they would appear again and ask for their money and they always went away spitting and snarling in a high old rage when you threw their goods at them. We were only there for a couple of hours and it was a relief to get away again.
Tonight we are passing up that famous ditch-The Suez Canal. Just at sunset as we were sailing through the Suez Canal I saw an Arab kneeling on his prayer rug on one of the lonely sandbanks. The rug was thrown down in front of his tent and he was facing Mecca as he went through the various gestures familiar to those of the Mohammedan faith; several camels standing near him added to the picturesque setting of the scene.

I saw my first mirage today when we were passing along the marshy portion of the canal before it leads into the desert itself. The images kept fading and reappearing in the shimmering heat waves. I have seen quite a few Arabs along the canal banks and I think that those that are wearing black robes must be Bedouins. The desert looks hot and cruel and it seems no wonder that it breeds a race of people who are hard and cruel as well. Tonight as I write this we are anchored in the Bitter Lakes but by morning we will be out into the Red Sea. *They had not been informed at Port Said that we had been delayed at Gibraltar and rumor had it that we had been bombed and sunk by General Franco of the Spanish Fascists, or rather by his planes.*

July 16th/38—The Red Sea and Marconi Sahib

The weather is very hot and stuffy but it won't be long now before we will be into the Indian Ocean and Monsoon weather. My "*boy*" gravely assures me that I will be unable to save any money out on the Indian Coast as everything costs so much. His statement is pretty well verified by what the Officers tell me and by what I have heard from the other chaps that have been out there. Apparently all I will have after two years isolation is the experience but that should be worth something.

I am getting used to being addressed by the Indians as *"Sahib"* now. Each Officer has a different name in Hindustani; *the Mate is known as "Burra Marlim Sahib"; the 2nd Mate as "Majla Marlim Sahib"; the 3rd Matre as "Sajla Marlim Sahib"* and I am known as *"**Marconi Sahib**"*etc. We get a few curry and rice dishes on here and I rather like it; it nearly burns your tongue off though when you are not used to it.

July 18th/38—Indian Ocean.

We are in a heavy monsoon gale and the ship is plunging so that the propeller races at times as it is thrown clear of the water. Spray is flying up about my cabin here on the boat-deck and the wind is howling a right mournful dirge. Everything movable insists on rolling abut the deck of my cabin.

July 21st/38

The storm weather has abated and life is as usual. We will soon be sighting Ceylon now and I am looking forward to my first glimpse of the Indies. The "Old Man" rather amuses us at times with his list of mostly imaginary ailments that he insists are bothering him.

The Mates claim that it is merely that he has nothing much to do except to worry about himself but they do not tell the "Old Man" that of course. The chief engineer is a very elderly Scotchman who never sees a joke at the proper time. Despite his age he is as spry as any of us and he always has his pipe going strong.

July 24th/38

Tonight the air is heavily scented with spice and the smell of the jungle. The lights of Galle, Ceylon, are visible in the distance. We are not calling at Colombo but are going straight to Calcutta.

July 28th/38

At tiffin(tea) time we picked up the Hugli river Pilot from off the Pilot Vessel at the mouth of the river. The Pilot vessel was a trim looking yacht—like ship and the pilot put out from her in a boat with Lascar oarsmen who looked quite smart in their blue uniforms with red sashes. They used the short and effective oar-stroke in rowing that is known as the Calcutta stroke and they soon covered the intervening space and the pilot crawled up the swaying pilot ladder on to our ship. It is about ninety miles up the river to Calcutta.

July 29th/38

We are traveling up the muddy Hugli River today and will reach Calcutta this evening. The river is very muddy and though it is a branch of the sacred Ganges I am not much taken with it. There seems to be lot of dead goats, cattle, etc. floating down it and they say that half burned bodies from the burning ghats are not an uncommon sight. The land along the river is very flat with many palm groves and paddy (rice) fields. There are a myriad of different styled river craft about here. Some are large high-sterned boats with sharp low bows and they look very awkward. The Indians stand up and face forward to row and they seem to keep time to a chant. I saw what looked like haystacks floating down the river by themselves but closer inspection revealed that they had those queer shaped boats previously mentioned underneath all the hay. They were apparently on their way to Calcutta as well. We have been swinging in close to the shore in places and there seem to be natives everywhere. The mud huts with their thatched roofs look rather picturesque under the palm trees.

July 30/38—Calcutta, India

Here we are in the second largest city in the British Empire and Indians seem to swarm everywhere. I have never seen so many beggars or quite so much dirt as this before. About every second Indian seems to either want to sell you something at twice its proper price or else he salaams you and wants bakshish. Holy hump-backed Indian cattle wander leisurely along the streets and everything has to go around them. There are many water buffalo pulling large wooded wheeled carts along as well as many ox carts drawn by ordinary oxen. The water buffalo are black in color with curving horns that generally curve inwards. The crowds of natives are certainly interesting to watch and they seem to get just as big a kick out of watching a white man. Deep gutters run along the streets and the Indians nonchalantly squat alongside them and use the gutters instead of lavatories. Some people may rave about the spicy smells of the East but all I have smelled up to date is the sickening smell of human urine around here, no wonder they die young in this country.

July 31st/38.

It is the rainy season here now and one has to duck around places between showers and it is very hot and sultry. These Bengali Indians dress in cheap cotton material that consists of a loose shirt and a sort of shirt that is pulled up between their legs. It is always white (or once was) and looks very sloppy but no doubt it is cool. They all carry umbrellas and chew and spit betel nut. The streets are stained red with betel juice and most Indians have a red smear across their face and their teeth are black from it. No one seems to use the sidewalks, they just swarm anywhere and the crowd just automatically opens and closes to let a taxi or an ox cart pass through. Not only is the crowd large but they have a smell all of their own even without the addition of the gutters. The average Indian seems to always be shouting or screaming about something and the noise that a crowd of them makes is terrific.

August 3rd/38 (Rug Buying Expert)

We are in Kidderpore Docks now and the barges that are alongside us smell to high heaven. The other night the 2nd. Engineer asked me if I would like to come with him through the bazaars as he was going to buy a rug for his wife. He said that his wife had coached him for hours on rug buying and if I wanted to learn something about rugs I should just watch him so I told him to lead on. We wandered from one bazaar to another until about 2a.m in the morning and I was getting dashed fed up with it all when at last the 3rd found what he wanted. He half unrolled the rug to show me all about it and almost gave me another lecture on rug buying. The next day when the rug was delivered he unrolled it to its full length and found that the other end was made of entirely different and very inferior material. He went back to the shop and of course raised quite a row but you can never get your money back from an Indian and the best that he was able to do was to get the shop keeper to exchange the rug for a lot of carved woodwork and stuff that will make grand dust collectors. I would hate to hear what his wife will say when she sees it all. Anyway he has not offered to give me anymore lessons in rug buying. Apparently one has to be in India for some time to be able to buy anything without getting hopelessly gypped.

August 4th/38 (Indian Football Game)

This afternoon I went to see a football game between an English regiment and an Indian Regiment. When I arrived at the European enclosure I was told that all the tickets had been sold but the chap at the gate told me to go on in anyway and so I saved about three Rupees! When I arrived back at the ship I learned that the other chaps had all been trying to buy tickets for the same game but could not get them I had a job to make them believe that I had walked in for nothing. The football game itself was very good but I was more interested in the crowds. All of Calcutta seems to turn out for a game like that and as the rich Indians are allowed into the European stands, I had a chance to study them at close quarters. The regimental Majors, Captains and other officers and the wild enthusiasm of the crowd all helped to make it a most interesting scene. There were a lot of Indian policemen about with their red turbans and long staffs and there was also a white Police sergeant. The Indian Sepoys and the English soldiers were along the sides of the field.

August 9th/38:

I signed off the **S/S Contractor** today at the shipping office and on to the **S/S Indora.** It was a fine new 6,622 ton vessel belonging to the British India Steam Navigation Company. She is a coastal cargo ship and was just brought out from England about two months ago. I am very fortunate in getting such a good ship. The British India Company is the largest shipping company in the East and the second largest shipping company in the British Empire.

August 10th/38

We are leaving Calcutta tonight bound for Colombo, Ceylon and I am looking forward to seeing it. I have a good cabin and radio office on the bridge deck with new radio gear. There are plenty of *"boys"* on here to wait on one so it looks as though I'm in for a leisurely life.

August 14th/38—(At Sea)

I am certainly pleased with this ship, the food is the best I have had at sea and it is available in overwhelming quantities. We get early morning tea, toast and fruit at about seven o'clock; breakfast at nine o'clock and it is excellent; a large glass of lime juice at eleven; tiffin at one o'clock' dinner at seven in port and at six at sea and then there is a late supper consisting of tea, sandwiches, etc, if you want it while at sea. My *"boy"* fortunately understands a bit of English but I am rapidly picking up a bit of the necessary Hindustani.

August 16th/38. Anchored in the bay here at Colombo tonight. The air smells very spicy and the shore is rimmed with palm trees. Across the bay a great neon sign flashes on and off. It reads "Ceylon for good tea". I will try it tomorrow when I go ashore.

August 20th/38 (Onshore—Ceylon—Lesson in the Ways of the East)

Today the 5th Engineer and I went out to Mount Lavinia which is a well known tourist resort. There is a beautiful palm lined beach with the pounding of the surf on the beach to add to the atmosphere of tropical fascination. We had tea there and then roamed about the surrounding countryside through palm groves and paddy fields where the natives were cutting the ripe grain.

From the sailor's point of view Colombo is a very expensive port as so many tourists come here and the natives are used to charging them about fifty percent extra on everything they buy. There are many Indians here who do most of the manual labor as the Sinhalese regard themselves as a bit above that. The Sinhalese are much more likable than the Indians. The rickisha wallas are all Indians and a greater bunch of rogues never lived. The first afternoon that the 5th and I went ashore our rickshaw walla tried to charge us about 95% too much and indignantly refused the correct fare offered them by the 5th. He calmly pocketed it again and walked away followed by howls of rage from the rickshaw wallas. I felt horribly embarrassed as we walked along the street with the rickshaw wallas howling at our elbows but the fiver who was an old hand at the game, took it all as a matter of course. Apparently the game is to get a large crowd around the poor embarrassed tourist so that he will gladly pay anything in order to get away. We walked along for a few blocks with the rickisha wallas at our elbows and in the end they were glad to take whatever we were willing to give them—and thus ended my first lesson in the ways of the East. If a chap on the Indian Coast attempted to pay tourist rates for everything he would not be able to live.

At Mount Lavinia we visited the lace factory where the Sinhalese girls make lovely lace. Not being experts in lace however, and sensing tourist prices the Fiver and I did not invest in lace. We also went for a stroll in the surrounding country among the paddy fields. We went quite a distance and when we saw a native thumbing his knife rather suggestively and looking at us a bit hard we decided to turn back—no doubt he thought we were tax collectors. As we were walking back to the hotel we became thirsty so we went into a cottage along the way and asked for a drink. The Sinhalese who seemed to own the house was very courteous and he immediately sent his boy to climb one of the tall palms in front of his cottage and he came back with several coconuts. They cut the top off of each one and there was as cool and as nice a drink as one would want. We had to make ourselves understood by using sign language as they only spoke Sinhalese. We gave them some bakshish and as far as we could make out parted as good friends.

August 24th/38

I went ashore and wandered about alone today. With hundreds of curious natives watching every move that one makes I am beginning to realize how the poor isolated Chinese must feel in Canada. These beggars never cease to watch one and wherever you look there are native eyes upon you. Today I hired a rickisha walla to take me out to the Cinnamon Gardens. I don't know why they call them that because there are only a few small cinnamon trees there. It is a very beautiful spot and as I sat in my rickisha and we twisted and turned along the narrow road among the tall stately palms and clumps of bamboo. I felt that it was well worth traveling so far to see so much beauty. After the Cinnamon Gardens I was pounced upon by a Sinhalese guide and then I had to part with my shoes and socks at the entrance as the Buddhists claim that it is very sacred ground—and who am I to argue with them! Inside the temple there was a large wooden image of a reclining Buddha. The guide was very glib with his description of it all and no doubt I was supposed to be very impressed—but I wasn't. In fact I kept thinking how foolish I would look wandering around a church barefooted in Canada! After we left the temple the self-appointed guide apparently thought it would be all right to charge me treble on account of me being an unbeliever—but fortunately I am beginning to get wise to the greedy ways of the East.

Another time the Fiver and I again visited the Cinnamon Gardens and while there visited the orchid house. The Fiver looked them all over and then demanded the reason why there were no **Dandelion Orchids**. The head gardener had been following us around with an eye on some praise and some bakshish and so was greatly taken back when he found that were greatly annoyed at his not having any dandelions. Apparently he had not heard of dandelions before and he promised to look into the matter. We solemnly assured him that he could not expect bakeshish if he could not show us dandelions after we had traveled so many miles to see them! It was a pleasure to see that the east could be bluffed a bit instead of the poor gullible tourist or easygoing sailor.

Part 2
1938

August 30th/38 (River Pilot)

We picked up our pilot from the Sandhead's pilot vessels this morning. It is about seventy-five miles up the Hughli river to Calcutta. The river is very treacherous as it is always silting up and occasionally a ship runs aground in it. The pilots are very good however and are world famous among the pilot services and it used to be one of the best jobs going. The Indian government is now insisting that Indians be taken into the service and of course the service is beginning to suffer as they have not yet had adequate training. Of course it was very interesting watching the many various types of river craft as we went up. The largest craft would be about fifteen tons and I should imagine and they have great high sterns and bows that are just slightly above the water. Could not get over the fact that most of the oarsmen stood up to row and kept walking back and forth to give the oars a wide sweep. Sometimes they were aided by large triangular sails, some of them white in color and others brown. At times we passed rather close to shore and had a good look at the wattled huts under the palm trees and the paddy fields with their mud walls that serve to keep the fields flooded.

September 1st/38 (Eden Gardens)

We are anchored at the Esplanade Moorings just off the Eden Gardens. The latter is a very well kept park with many fine palms, clumps of bamboo and other tropical woods. There are also many flowering shrubs and trees and the lily ponds are very nice—some of the lily pads are by far the largest I have ever seen; they are often about five feet across and turn up all around the edges and the flowers are white and pink. Carrion crows seem to fairly fill the trees and their mournful croaking seems to fill the hot humid air. I am rather disappointed that there are none of the brilliantly plumaged birds that I thought to see in the tropics.

The crowds are certainly colorful here even if they are a bit smelly. Any amount or any lack of dress among the natives seems to be quite all right. Some are content to wear the minimum amount of loin cloth and to let an ample amount of cow-dung smeared over their foreheads make up the rest of their outfit. The most common dress around here however appears to be the cheap white linen skirts which the Bengali pulls up between his legs. It looks very untidy but I suppose it is cool. Every Indian seems to carry an umbrella and when it is not raining they use them to keep the hot sun off. These people seem to sleep everywhere both day and night. They sprawl under the shade of the trees along the sidewalks; they sleep under the archways fronting their shops, in fact one has to often watch his step to avoid stepping on sleeping natives as you walk along. They usually just pull a dirty old linen sheet up over their heads and they look like a bunch of corpses stretched out. At night they sometimes hire cheap wooden beds and sleep out along the road. Everyone seems to chew betel-nut, men, women and children; it stains their lips red and their teeth black. The roads and sidewalks are certainly red from it. At almost every corner is a pan-seller who either squats along the sidewalk with his pan-leaves, betel-nut and lime or else sits cross-legged on the counter of his little shop.

September 6th/38

We shifted to our present berth in Kidderpore Docks the other day. The weather is certainly hot and sultry and it makes one feel very languid. Today the 5th Engineer and I went for a walk among the thousands of bazaars that stretch for miles along here. Every second Indian must keep a shop from the number of shops that there are and it made me wonder how they could all make a living. However the streets were certainly crowded with natives and after all they can live quite nicely on a few annas worth of rice per day. We walked far back into gloomy covered bazaars, no doubt we were the first white men to go wandering so far into them. I must say that most of the Indian goods offered for sale in the ordinary bazaars are pretty crude ware. There is much clay pottery, no end of cheap Japanese goods and I think it would take quite an expert to tell the good stuff from the bad stuff in such a place. The Indians certainly would never tell any-one.

I think the smells will long remain my most vivid memory of India. As one walks along the streets the smells assail one from everywhere; there is the stench from the garbage that is thrown out into the streets; there are fra-grant perfumes from the shops; there is the appetizing smell of roasting corn as it roasts over the charcoal brazier of the roast corn seller on the street corner and the ever present smell of human urine caused by unsani-tary habits. There were many twelve and thirteen year old girls carrying children about and I suppose that they were their own as this is the coun-try of child marriages. There we many sturdy looking Sikhs and Gurkhas wandering about the bazaars. They wear more clothing than the southern Indian, are much fairer in complexion and often carry business-like dag-gers at their sides. We watched one rag and cow-dung covered fakir walk-ing along calling a half grown heifer after him—no doubt he would be considered a very holy man indeed. There were many holy cattle (*of the hump back type)* numerous goats, many pariah dogs and chickens about the streets.

September 7th/38 (Loading coal)

Last night must have been some sort of native holiday because there were native tom-toms beating everywhere. Sometimes the Indians sang at the same time and that was worse still because the "harmony"sounds as though you were stomping on a cat's tail—the same mournful howl results.

We are loading coal for Rangoon and dozens of coolies of both sexes walk up the ship's gangways with heavy baskets of coal on their heads. They form an endless chain and they toss their coal into the bunkers as they go past. They are a spindly legged bunch and they make me wonder how they can stand such toil in the hot sun. Of course if machinery was used instead these people would simply have to starve. Despite it all they seem fairly happy as they are always laughing and jabbering among themselves.

September 13th/38 (Rangoon, Burma: Shwe Dagon Pagoda and Sampans)

We arrived here yesterday from Calcutta and are now at mooring in the great Irrawaddy River opposite the gilded Botataung Pagoda. Rangoon here is about forty miles up from the sea. On both sides of the river coming up it was mostly flat paddy (rice) land for as far as one could see. There were occasional palm groves and many small white pagodas, each pagoda was set on its own little hilltop and they looked very picturesque. As we drew near Rangoon the famous Shwe Dagon Pagoda came into sight. It stands on a hill near the city and the pagoda itself is three hundred and sixty-eight feet high and can be seen for quite a distance. It is said to be about 2500 years old and I am looking forward to visiting it.

The river seemed to be filled with queer looking Burmese craft called sampans and at the city here there are swarms of them. I am told that they hold about two passengers with a fair amount of safety but they look pretty flimsy to me. The stern is about three and a half feet wide and the bow is narrow and curves up high into the air and sometimes they curve right back in a sort of semi-circle. The passengers sit near the front while the Sampan walla stands up in the back to scull these strange looking craft along. He faces the bow to scull and everything sort of depends on his sense of balance and his skillful handling of those oars. The river is tidal here and very swift and the oars are only tied on with rope so it doesn't look very safe. Most of the sampans are painted in brilliant colors and many of the sampan wallas wear bark hats with broad rims and pointed conical tops to protect them from the rain. Speaking of rain it has been pouring at regular intervals ever since our arrival and it pours down by the bucketful.

September 15th/38—Rangoon, Burma.

It stopped raining for a while yesterday and the 5th Engineer and I went ashore in one of the sampans. I felt as though we were riding on a toboggan on very icy snow; owing to the strong current in the Irrawaddy they are made to draw as little water as possible and that is the only reason that they can be rowed against the current. The current is so swift most of the time that only an excellent swimmer could keep afloat in it. We landed at a jetty near the Botataung Pagoda and wandered about the pagoda for a while taking snaps. Then we hired a rickshaw and went rolling along in grand style up to the Suley Pagoda which is near the center of the town. We noticed that there are really more Indians and Chinese here in Rangoon than there are Burmese.

September 16th/38 (Rangoon—Curry and Rice)

Last night I went ashore with our Indian 3rd Officer who took me to the Bombay Restaurant for a feed of Curry and rice. The curry was so hot that I could feel my scalp tingling. We then went to a show and after that visited Murgi Street which is famous for it's Indian style chicken dinners. It is one of the places to go when in Rangoon. Along the street were many Indian cooks who had tables along the side of the street as well as booths along the side of a mosque. We were served with a plate of grilled bits of chicken, chicken livers, a large plate of sliced onion cooled off with vinegar with green peppers added, a large plate of paraties each (these are flat rice cakes and are quite doughy) and a dish full of curry to dip the chicken and paraties into. No knives, forks or spoons were supplied and we ate Indian fashion—with our fingers. It was quite a novelty to me and I rather enjoyed it except for the fact that I could see that the Indian cooks were using their fingers just as freely in getting the food ready. However no one seems to know anything about germs in this country and you just live or you die—kismet.

An Indian only uses his right hand to eat with and Charlie (our nickname for the third) was an expert at it. He told me that they ate their food off of green banana leaves at his home in the south of India. Charlie is very dark but he seems a real gentleman in every way and is accepted as one of us on board. His only failing is drinking a bit too much and feeling a bit sorry for himself at times. He told me that he ate that way at home as he did not want to offend his mother by making her think that he had departed too much from Indian ways. Anyway we had a very successful Indian evening even though I am suffering from indigestion today.

September 18th/38 (Rangoon, Burma—Shwe Dagon Pagoda)

Today the 3rd Officer, the 5th Engineer and myself visited the **Shwe Dagon Pagoda.** Arriving there we had to leave our shoes and socks at the entrance to one of the large covered stairways that lead up to the pagoda grounds. As the grounds are considered holy by the Buddhists a quick way to start a riot is to try and wear your shoes near one of their pagodas. The stairway was long and steep and there were many pretty Burmese girls selling flowers as most worshipers buy some to leave as an offering before the idols. At the top the great bulk of the *Shwe Dagon* seemed to tower above everything. It has a huge base that is about fourteen hundred feet in circumference at the bottom and which gradually tapers up into a tall graceful spire. The large base portion of the pagoda is covered with gold-leaf while the spire portion is covered with solid gold. At the top is a cupola that is hung with little bells that tinkle every time the breeze blows; the cupola is studded with precious and semi-precious jewels. Several years ago an earthquake shook spire and cupola from the top of the pagoda and the jewels were scattered far and wide but it is said that every jewel was returned. A new spire was put on and the old one stands in another portion of the pagoda grounds.

I was under the impression that one could go inside the *Shwe Dagon* but like other pagodas it is built of either solid brick or stone. Around the base of the *Shwe Dagon* are many small gilded pagoda; many of these have temples built in front of them and contain Buddha images made out of stone and brass. Around the broad roadway that circles the large pagoda are numerous temples that contain many more large and small images made out of alabaster and brass. Others contain priceless Buddha relics and others precious jewels and other gifts that have been made to the pagoda. Many of the temple roofs were the duplicates in iron work of the fine old Burmese woodcarving that made their temples so unique in design. In the temple was hung a large forty-two and a half ton bell. It is very thick and inside there is room for half a dozen men to stand upright. When the British first annexed Lower Burma they attempted to remove the bell to Calcutta. Just as they were putting it on the deck of the ship it slipped and fell to the bottom of the muddy and swift flowing Irrawaddy.

SHWEDAGON PAGODA OVERLOOKS RANGOON AND IRRAWADDY RIVER

The British Engineers could not raise it as every attempt only ended in failure. The Burmese then asked the British if they might keep the bell in their own country if they could recover the bell. The British smiled at the thought of the Burmese being able to succeed and granted their request. The Burmese by using floats made of hollow bamboo raised the bell and removed it to the *Shwe Dagon*.

We trotted around in our bare feet and perspired freely in the hot sun, the hot roadway burned our feet as we went and I envied the Burmese walking nonchalantly along as though you couldn't fry an egg on it. It was well worth it and with the endless stream of worshipers coming and going it was rather a colorful sight. The neat looking little Burmese women and girls with flowers in their hair and wearing white lace blouses and gaily colored lungyis(skirts) were very easy to look at; the only thing being that many of them were smoking about nine to ten inch white cigars and it looked a bit odd to me at first. The cigars are about an inch thick and they seem to be very popular among both the Burmese men and women. We had a job to convince our tourist wise guide that we were not sticking Rupees in every available crack and cranny "just for luck" as he gravely explained. After we had convinced him that it would be "bad luck" for us he seemed quite resigned to it. We could just imagine him paddling back after the tourists had left to fish out all the odd coins they had left "just for luck".

Many of the worshipers sat before the images and howled in a loud and mournful manner; the women and girls left bunches of flowers before the alters and the Pungyis (Buddhist monks) that wandered around dressed in their orange robes did not seem to do anything much.

At the end of several hours wandering about the call of hunger became a bit stronger than the call of the temple bells so we descended the long stairway, collected our foot gear and proceeded to the mission out at the Royal Lakes. At the lakes we first had some lunch and then went sailing in one of the sailing boats. The Royal Lakes are right near the *Shwe Dagon*.

Our sailing was not overly successful as the breeze died down just when we reached the center of the lake and when it came time to return we had to row back but we enjoyed it all. The Fiver had to return to the ship as he was on night watch so the 3rd and I went to the pictures and then to the Bombay restaurant where we had curried chicken and rice. It was midnight and the streets were deserted as we returned to the ship. The bare feet of the rickisha walla pattered on the pavement as he trotted along and only that and the crickets broke the silence of the night. At the jetty we picked a sampan out of the multitude offered and as we skimmed along over the water, on our way to the ship, we decided that it had been a most enjoyable day.

September 20/38—Rangoon, Burma

The many barges with their large triangular brown and white sails are always nice to watch. Many tugs puff along pulling long rafts of teak logs to the sawmills along the river bank. At times we can hear the high shrill whine of the saws as they eat through the large teak logs. There are many ocean going ships from various parts of the world tied up to river moorings the same as we are. The barge wallas are all Indians and most of them wear only loin-cloths. There are usually four men and a boy to do their cooking on each barge. The barges are clustered all around the ship and it is interesting to watch the barge wallas below as they prepare their curry and rice. They pound the various spices and peppers up into a powder for their curry. The rice looks white and fluffy from the deck and no doubt the curry would be about the hottest stuff out. They sit around in a circle to eat it and use only their fingers to scoop up the rice. They use only the right hand to eat with.

There are many river boats belonging to the Irrawaddy Flotilla Company and most of the larger ones are paddle wheel craft. The Mandalay cargo boat that leaves every evening has a large "flat" or barge on each side of it. In the flats are regular trade stores as well as general cargo. Both the Mandalay express and the cargo steamers leave from the Botatoung Jetty which is opposite. They have steamers running to Prome, Bassein and many other river ports. The weather is very humid and I have to have my boy brush all my shoes and blue clothing off almost every day to keep the blue mold from forming on them. The sunsets on the river here are the best I have ever seen; the monsoon clouds seems to break away just enough to make the effect almost perfect. The river twists in such a manner at this particular spot that it is running almost due east and west and the sails of the many barges stand out in silhouette against the setting sun. At the same time most of our native crew (Mohammedans only) can be seen on the poop saying their evening prayers and the same thing is being done on many of the barges at the same time. All told they are most fascinating evenings with the beauty of the sunsets and so much of interest to see.

September 23rd/38 (Rangoon)

We listened to the Queen launching the Queen Elizabeth at the Clyde and thought she did it very nicely. Afterwards we elected the 3rd to go ashore and bring us all back chicken and paraties from Murghi Street. When he came back we sat down on the deck and everyone dug in Indian style—hands only and no knives or forks allowed. We are all wondering if we will soon be at war with Germany, it certainly looks a lot like it.

September 30th/38—Rangoon, Burma (Shirley Temple Wood work!)

This morning I went ashore before breakfast so as to have a look around the market before it started to rain as it always does in the afternoon. I took my camera along to take a few snaps and at the market I was immediately mistaken for a press photographer by several shopkeepers who wanted me to take snaps of their shops. They asked me where I came from and on learning it was from Canada they were more certain than ever that I was one—probably because they had never heard of such a place before. One Burmese shopkeeper begged me to take a picture of his shop front to prove to the people of America that the art of woodworking was not dead in Burma (all the interpreting was done by a young Burman who spoke good English) So we strolled over to his shop to see the wonderful Burmese woodwork and found that his most prized bit was—a fretwork cut-out of Shirley Temple. I had a job to keep from laughing but solemnly took a picture of it all. However I got my own back by insisting that his rather reluctant wife should be in the snap—just to prove to the people of America that Burmese women are free to own and keep shops the same as in America. Her husband had to do a lot of persuading as Burmese women are very shy but it was managed.

The Burmese market people were very interesting and the sight of a Burmese girl or woman smoking a great white cheroot never fails to amuse me. I took several snaps of them but had to do it when they were not looking as the country people in particular are very shy. There were all sorts of fruits and vegetables for sale such as mangoes, popiyas, small bananas, durians and mangosteens. A rickisha walla had been following me about all morning—these people simply cannot understand a white man wanting to walk, even for exercise—so I returned to the ship via rickisha.

Oct. 2/38—RANGOON, Burma

We are leaving here tomorrow. The cargo coolies keep up a steady chant both day and night as they stow the teak timbers down in the hold. At the Shwe Dagon the other day our guide held up a small stone before an alter and said that we should do the same and make a wish. However he did a lot of howling and wailing that we didn't. A customs officer told me today that as you hold the stone and make a wish and if the stone grows heavy in ones hand the wish is going to be granted, if the stone gets lighter the wish is not going to be granted—just bunkum no doubt.

At Sea, Bay of Bengal (Heavy Gale)

Heavy gale, all shore stations sending out gale warnings and my main and emergency transformer has burnt out. It is impossible to repair it at sea so my transmitters are useless. The ship is rolling heavily—hope nothing goes wrong with no radio.

Oct. 9th/38 (Kankesanturai, Ceylon

We arrived here at noon and just 24hours late owing to the storm. We are anchored off shore about a mile out. Will have to wait till we reach Colombo to get the set repaired.

Oct. 11th/38—Colombo, Ceylon—Arrived here this morning and Gov. Radio Inspector came and took the transformer away to be re-wound.

Oct. 12/38—Colombo, Ceylon-Radio Inspector returned the re-wound transformer today and set all OK again. Haven't had a chance to get around here this time. Just went for one walk among the bazaars and got lost.

Oct. 14/38—Trivandrum, India. Anchored offshore and all I can see is palm trees along the shore. The Indians come out through the heavy swell in frail looking dugout canoes. They take a few bags in each canoe and away they go.

Oct.15th/38—Cochin India. This is a fine harbor here and is surrounded by palm trees. There is an old and a new town here. The old town looks very interesting but we are not allowed to go there as there are several cases of plague. The new part is a fair ways away and as we are anchored out in the harbor and leaving tomorrow at noon I may not see it.

Oct. 19th/38—Bombay, India

Arrived here this morning and reported at the B.W.M.S. depot. I had to get ashore by launch as we are anchored out in the bay and unloading our cargo into lighters. The launch landed us at Ballar Pier and the depot is right near there. After finishing my business at the depot I wandered about the city for the rest of the afternoon and seemed to be lost most of the time but it was all quite interesting. The Indians seem to be a bit different than the Bengali Indian and if anything just a shade better dressed. There are many of the stalwart looking Indians from the north of Findia and small dark Indians from the Malabar Coast. Then there are many Parsees who originally came from Persia and who are sun-worshipers. They wear peculiar looking hats on their heads that are shaped like the hoof of a cow. When they die the bodies are removed to the Parsees tower and the sun and the crows and vultures do the rest. The bones are said to then drop down into a deep well underneath. The Parsees are great traders and most of them are very wealthy and they seem to have fine homes.

Oct. 21st/38—Bombay, India.

The bay here is very large and is surrounded by hills and Islands except for the city itself which is built on fairly level ground although the Parsees Tower of Silence is built on a good high hill. In the early morning when the sun is just rising and the water is as calm as a mill pond it is quite delightful but about noon it becomes hot enough that it makes one wish for a cooler clime. The famous Gateway to India stands just across the way in front of the Taj Hotel. The Hotel is supposed to be one of the finest but personally I cannot see anything very striking about it's design. India certainly appears to be an expensive country to get around in and things seem dear to buy as well. Indian people seem to live on next to nothing or else on a whole lot; there appears to be no happy medium.

Oct. 24th/38

We left Bombay tonight and are bound for Tuticorin and Calcutta. Tuticorin is on the southernmost tip of India.

October 29th/38—Tuticornin, India.

We arrived here yesterday and are anchored about a quarter of a mile from shore. Sailing boats are bringing the bales of cotton out from shore and they come out in a steady line. The shore looks flat and rather monotonous from here; there are a few palm trees but that looks to be about all. It has been raining a lot here; we will be leaving here in just a few hours now.

November 4th/38—Calcutta, India

Here we are back once more. It seems quite cool and pleasant here just now and the rains are about over with. I reported at the B.W.M.S. depot today so I am now free to look around. The place is no cleaner than usual but I think I am getting used to it now and also used to seeing naked children running around the streets, etc. The leprous beggars that insist on sticking their sores under one's nose are disgusting and the cripples and blind beggars seem to swarm the streets. They say that many of the beggars are deliberately deformed as children so that they can earn their living in that way. Nothing would surprise me anymore after some of the things that I have seen.

November 5th/38

Tonight the 2nd Officer Donald Sleigh and I went to the pictures then to Firpo's for lunch and then later we drifted around to the Continental where we watched the cabaret show. There was a lot of the usual heavy drinking going on there and one party insisted on smashing their glasses on the floor after they finished each round of drinks.

November 8th/38—Calcutta, India

This morning the 2nd Officer and I visited the Victoria memorial. It is a beautiful building built of white marble and is much like the famous Taj Mahal in appearance. It's huge dome rises above the city and it's graceful lines just have to be admired even by the most inartistically inclined. Inside it there are many relics of the Victorian era as well as hundreds of paintings of the same period. The more I see of this country the more I realize that it was that Victorian era that really left a lasting mark upon India—far more so than the present day as far as the average Indian is concerned.

November 11th/38—Calcutta, India

I went up town today and watched the Armistice Day services that were held on the Maiden. It was a very colorful turnout with the Bengal Lancers, Indian Sepoys and the British regiments all taking part. The Governor was there and they laid wreaths. The flags and standards waved gaily in the breeze and the bands played and I think it was the Governor that spoke in a voice that no one could hear. The marching soldiers, the bugles and the bands were all very stirring and I thought how both Dad and Mother would probably enjoy it all had they been here.

November 12th/40

We left Calcutta today bound for Rangoon, Burma. We are now steaming down the Hughli River past the many mud huts under palm trees along the shore and the many paddy fields. We have a cargo of coal and will be about a couple of weeks unloading it.

November 16/38—Rangoon, Burma—Once more we are anchored or rather moored out near the center of the river. It is rather nice to see the pagoda again and on the river here it is always interesting to watch the many sampans, the tugs towing their teakwood rafts and the river steamers of the Irrawaddy Flotilla as well as the many barges with their large triangular sails.

November 20th/38—Rangoon, Burma.

The weather is quite warm during the day but is cool enough at night dropping to about seventy degrees Fahrenheit. The sunrise and the sunsets on the river here are really something worth while as they have all the necessary surroundings such as temples, pagodas, sails on the river, etc to really make them effective. Often in the stillness of early morning and evening the wood smoke from the many barges fills the air as the barge wallas cook their curry and rice. Strangely enough the fragrant smell of wood smoke always makes me slightly home sick.

November 25th/38—Moulmein, Burma.

The anchor chain rattled out through the hawse-pipe as we came to anchor off the beautiful, palm-clad town of Moulmein. Back of the town stretched a hill that ran parallel to the river. Along the top of the hill, standing silhouetted against the sky, stood several white pagodas. At the far end of the hill we could see a golden pagoda surrounded by many temples. The Chief Engineer, who was standing by my side, started to hum the words of Kipling's immortal *"Mandalay"* and I wondered just which pagoda could be the *"Old Moulmein Pagoda, lookin' lazy at the sea"*. Moulmein here is about thirty miles up the Salween River and the palm clad and sleepy little town stretches along the river bank.

Soon the work of loading our cargo of teakwood and rice began, accompanied by the incessant rattling of our winches and the chanting of our cargo coolies. The Second Officer and I decided to escape from the noise of cargo work for the afternoon by going ashore so we hailed one of the queer-shaped Burmese sampans passing by and shortly we were stepping ashore at one of the river jetties. It was hot and sultry ashore so we looked about for some method of conveyance. There were several Madras gharry—wallas about with their Victorian looking carriages and little ponies so we jumped into a gharry and were soon whirling along through the crowded streets to the bazaar.

We found the bazaar to consist of many buildings that sprawled along the river front in a haphazard sort of way. In one corner of the bazaar we found piles of bark hats; they had wide slanting brims and their pointed tops were tipped with tin. A cheerful little Burman, who spoke excellent English, told us that the bark hats were mostly worn by the river boatmen and the paddy field workers during the monsoon season. We strolled on and came to the cheroot portion of the bazaar where cheroots of all lengths and sizes were for sale; some of them were made up with the black strong-smelling tobacco that places the Burmese cheroot in a class by itself the world over while the cheroots that were more favored for local consumption were made of chopped up tobacco rolled in white corn husks. Many of the cheroots were as long as eight inches and it is rather startling to see a dainty little Burmese maiden calmly puffing away at such an over-sized cigar, for in Burma the women are just as heavy smokers as the men. We walked on into another section of the market and discovered much in the way of Burmese handicrafts. There were finely carved alabaster images of Buddha, beautiful Burmese parasols, hand carved ivory work, and rows of wicked looking Burmese dahs that were all bright and shiny and ready for use.

November 28th/38—Moulmein, Burma

Today the 3rd Officer and I climbed the hill of the pagodas that overlook the town and the surrounding country. It was in the afternoon that we climbed the steep path that leads up to the top to the foot of one of the white pagodas. Along the summit runs a roadway and along this we walked to see the other pagodas. It was a grand view down over the river that stretched into the distance. The hills that lay about Moulmein are very peculiar as they seem to have been dropped into the center of the flat paddy fields and are very high and steep—each hill seems to have one or two pagodas on it's summit. It was very quiet and peaceful along the hilltop; the silence was broken only by the sounds from the town below, the tinkling of the little bells that hung in the cupolas of the pagodas and the occasional sound of a gong being struck in the monastery by the golden pagoda. We met a few Buddhist monks walking along the pathway but otherwise we were undisturbed. At sunset with the sun sunk down over the river coloring the river and the sky with shades of orange and yellow it seemed as though we were in another world. It was so peaceful and quiet along the hill that I regretted having to leave.

December 2nd/38—Moulmein, Burma—(Jungle hunting for tigers, pigs, and jungle fowl)

I have just arrived back from a hunting trip into the Burmese jungle with Captain Wordingham and it was a wonderful trip. We left on November 29th and had the Police Inspector's car to go in. He is a friend of the Captains and although he was unable to go with us he insisted that we at least take his car and sent along his Burmese cook to do our cooking. Not content with that he sent along his Chinese-Burman Sub-Inspector to act as our guide and interpreter so we are really much indebted to him. We left Moulmein early in th morning and sped along the road that leads to the Siamese border. About eleven o'clock we climbed up through a high range of hills where the road made several corkscrew turns and then not far on the other side we stopped at a crude sort of a tea room where we had some very thick tea and watched the naked children scrambling about and listened to the Burmese arguing with Chit Hlaing our guide as to the best hunting grounds. Leaving there we passed through low jungle country with the occasional village surrounded by paddy fields.

In the afternoon we reached the village of Kyain Seikgyi and the home of one Saw Tun Nyein, a Karin Christian and a friend of our guide. This person was a well-to-do landowner and had a large house. The Karin's are one of the Burmese tribes who are more westernized than most of them, also their skin is much lighter than most Burmese. Like nearly all the Burmese homes the floor was about nine feet off the ground and we went up a stairway to get into it. There were chairs and tables there in western style and the landowner's wife and his mother offered us tea while we waited for some more Burmese hunters to come along.

When the other hunters came along we all started off on foot for an afternoon's hunt as there was plenty of jungle right around there. The landowner came along as well as he was a keen hunter. After crossing the Aami River we stopped at a jungle hut for a rest. There we had to climb up a ladder to the first floor and sat down on the bamboo matting. We were offered popyias (a tropical fruit) and betel nut to chew. We had some popyias but declined the betel nut with thanks. The owner of this hut was a poor man yet by way of contrast with a poor Indian's habitation the hut was clean and though obviously poor the Burman did not hesitate to offer whatever hospitality he had.

We descended from the hut and continued on our way. By this time several more beaters had joined us and as we went along several men left their work in the paddy fields to join us and several Burmese girls came along to help beat the jungle as well. Soon we reached a large patch of jungle and one old hunter showed us where to stand along the trail and then the beaters circled out around the patch of jungle and started closing in and beating the bushes with sticks and dahs to make a noise and scare any animals towards us as they came. They told us that we could expect either ghi(a small deer) or wild pig along with plenty of jungle fowl. The latter are the ancestors of our domestic poultry.

We were using double-barrel shotguns with one barrel loaded with SG shot for the deer and the other with finer shot for the jungle fowl. We did several patches of jungle in that way before sunset and we got several jungle fowl. A ghi dashed out of the long grass along the trail where the Old Man was standing and nearly ran him down. He was so startled that he missed it completely much to his chagrin. The beaters gathered round and had a good old laugh about it and I tried to look sympathetic. One of the Burmese hunters shot a ghi just as we were finishing the last beat much to everyone's delight. It was a bit strange standing beside some jungle path at sunset and listening to the shouts of the beaters as they drew nearer. The shadows soon lengthened and it grew much cooler. The parrots screamed and chattered in the tree-tops as they settled down on their roosting places for the night and the jungle thrushes gave us their last evening song.

Hunting in Burma

Before we started to hunt the Hunters made an opium offering to the God of the hunters. Here they are making the offering in the stockade surrounding a Headman's hut in a jungle village. Here we had tiffin before starting our hunt.

After a tiresome beat we would sit and rest while waiting for stragglers to join us. The hardy little Burmese beaters are merry fellows and always eager for a hunt or a joke.

ox cart trail.

This is the usual jungle hut in Lower Burma. The floor is 5 or 6 feet off the ground as a protection against dangerous animals The framework is built from bamboo and the roof and walls are thatched leaves

It was bright moonlight as we started walking back and it was just as well as we had a long way to walk. There was the steady hum of a myriad of insects and fireflies lit the shadows. By the time we had been ferried across the river again the Old Man was demanding an ox cart to go the rest of the way to the village in as he was tired. So Chit Hlaning called at several huts as we went and at length found a place where they had an ox cart. The oxen were yoked up and we climbed into the cart and bumped along on our way to town—my first ox cart ride.

In about an hour we reached the town where we had left the car and so left our ox cart. We stopped in front of a shop to buy some cold drinks and it was interesting watching the many Burmese along the street. There were naked children, young men dressed in their best lungyis (skirt that is worn by both men and women in Burma) and pretty girls with flowers in their black hair and wearing white lace blouses. Chit Hlaning appeared to be very popular among the villagers and from what I could make out he was telling them some pretty tall yarns about our hunting. The village people all seemed a happy lot and the more I saw of them during my trip the more I liked the Burmese people. They are an independent lot and not given to mixing much with other races and I like them for that; they are not very fond of hard work either and I think they are quite right there as well.

Arriving back at the landowner's place we had a late dinner and slept there for the night. Early the next morning a bus arrived packed full of beaters. We had hired the bus as we were going over a little used road back into the jungle where we were going to stay for a couple of days. We managed to squeeze in amongst them without guns and camp equipment and away we went. We passed through the jungle and out onto the rough jungle trail and believe me it was rough. The ox carts that had passed over it during the rainy season had left ruts that were much too wide for the tires of our bus and in places the water had washed deep gullies across the road. However we appeared to be prepared for all this as we had shovels in the bus and whenever necessary everyone turned out to shovel or to push as was required. We passed through teak plantations and jungle where willowy looking clumps of bamboo waved in the breeze.

At length we arrived at the end of the road and left the bus in front of a jungle hut. The bus driver had been going to return to town and come back for us but the road was so bad that he decided to come hunting with us instead. Several of the beaters set out to find an ox cart to carry our hunting gear in and the rest of us sat around and waited and talked to the women who lived in the near-by huts. They said that their men-folk were away working for a few days for the land owner. Each district has its well-to-do landowner or so who hires these poorer people for a few days each year. That bit of work plus their own little paddy field and the few fruits that they both have is quite enough to keep them—comfortably if not in luxury and it looks to me like an ideal life. The ox cart arrived and we piled our guns and baggage into it. The Old Man decided to ride on it as well but certain parts of my anatomy were still pretty sore from my ride of the previous evening so I decided to walk. In about a quarter of an hour or so we arrived at a small village and went to the Headman's huts. The Headman is apparently responsible to the Government for the collection of taxes and other Gov. Duties and he had the best house in the village. We climbed up the ladder that led to the first floor and they produced a couple of chairs for us while the others parked themselves on the bamboo matting. At this place we had our tiffin which consisted of curried chicken, rice and fruit. The Headman could speak a bit of Hindustani so he and the Old Man got on famously.

After the tiffin we started to walk to the jungle edge where we were to start our beat. The ox cart was to go on during the afternoon and we made our camp ready near a river that was some ways off. We were to finally end up there after the sun went down. We started hunting and Chit Hlaing assured us that there were tigers about and that the beaters might manage to drive one out. We were to try for the jungle fowl as well but I am afraid that I let a lot of them go because the thought of meeting a tiger with only one barrel loaded with SG shot and the other loaded with bird shot didn't appeal to me very much! I never did have much faith in shotguns anyway. The wild pigs are supposed to be pretty nasty things if you only wound them as well! I must confess that I kept a weather eye open for a convenient tree with low branches—just in case! Anyway it seemed that it was bad tiger and pig weather because none came hopping out during our many beats. Towards evening we shot quite a few jungle fowl. They are a dark brown bird and have purplish neck feathers and I can vouch for the fact that they are good to eat.

The Burmese jungle that we visited was not the great high jungle with the dank and dark undergrowth of the African jungle. The trees are mostly about fifty or sixty feet high and the trees do not grow so close together but the scrub and undergrowth of various kinds is very thick underneath. The jungle and villages and paddy fields seem to blend together. One moment you are in the jungle and the next in a small unexpected village.

Evening in the jungle is something to be remembered; the heat of the day rapidly gives way to the coolness of the night as the sun sinks like a huge ball of orange colored fire below the treetops. The long thirsty miles and their fatigue are rapidly forgotten and it seems as though one were suddenly living in another land. The parrots gradually cease their chattering in the tree tops and the jungle fowl cocks cease their crowing. As the shadows lengthen it seems as though all the world has paused for a period of silent meditation.

We camped that night on a teak log raft that was lying on the placid water of the river waiting for the monsoon floods to float it down the river to the saw mill. Someone had built a bamboo and palm thatched hut on it and it kept the heavy night dew off us. The ox cart had already arrived when we reached there. We slept (the Old Man and I) with our blankets thrown on the bamboo matting that had been placed over the logs. The Burmese did not worry about blankets and seemed quite happy uncovered even with the mosquitoes that nearly ate us up. As we were dropping off to sleep we heard an elephant trumpeting and the Burmese hunter told us it was a rogue elephant that had killed several people and damaged a lot of crops. It was on the other side of the stream but it seemed all too narrow after that as a shotgun does not make a very effective elephant gun in an emergency.

Early the next morning we waited for some of our Burmese hunters who had been out after wild pig all night. They arrived without pigs but with several green parrots that they said were good eating. We set out with the purpose of going pig hunting that day and in time came to a regular forest of elephant grass—have never seen such high grass before. It was as hot as an oven in that sea of grass and our shirts were soon soaked through and I could even feel the perspiration trickling down into my shoes. We hunted all morning without success and in the afternoon decided to try jungle fowl shooting for a change before we returned to our bus where the ox cart was to leave our supplies.

The jungle fowl hunt was quite successful that afternoon and we gave some birds to the beaters who had joined us as we went. The jungle Burmese love a hunt and they seemed to have a great old time laughing and chatting among themselves. They would sit smoking their long cheroots or bamboo pipes and Chit Hlaing would translate much of what they were saying to the Old Man and I. We parted with many of the beaters late that afternoon and returned to the bus with the remainder. We reached the town after dark that night and there took leave of the rest of the beaters and proceeded to the land-owner's house where we had another late dinner.

The next morning we said good-bye to our hosts and started back for Moulmein. Just after leaving the town again and a few miles along the way we came to a lake where we were going to try some duck shooting. The Old Man and Chit Hlaing went one way around it while another Burman and I went the other way. The ducks that flew up were too high for me to hit so we started back to join the others and passed quite close to a hut along the trail and an old bearded man was sitting or rather squatting as the Burmese always do and he was mixing the clay out of the path and fashioning it into rough bricks. I paused to watch him for a moment and nearly fell over backwards when he looked up and said *"Good morning Sir"* in perfect English. Then he added *"How are you this morning Sir and where do you come from?"*

I could hardly believe that it was that brown old man with the betel nut stained teeth and the red cloth wound round his head and a Lungyis about his waist that was speaking. I knew that few of these people could speak English so far back in the jungle and it certainly surprised me. I managed to stutter out that I was off a ship at Moulmen. *"And what country are you from?"* asked the old Burman. I told him I was from North America, Canada to be exact. *"I have also been to America"*, said the old Burman. *"I studied there for eight years"*. Then he added as if an afterthought *"I have still a very good friend in America."* I murmured that it was indeed surprising to find one who spoke such good English in this part of the jungle old Burman seemed to suddenly regret that he had said so much and graciously added *"I will think of America every day from now on"* then he resumed his task of mixing the clay with his hands as though I simply did not exist.

I stood rather helplessly for a moment wanting to ask him more about what he was doing there and a dozen or so other questions but his goodbye had been so gracious and so definite that I decided against it. With a last look back at the old Burman mixing clay by the side of the road I proceeded on my way. Was he really a Burman? I will often wonder about that; then too a Burman can seldom raise a few whiskers on his chin let along a beard. Perhaps he was really white? Neither Chit Hlaing or any of the other Burmese could tell me anything about him, or if they knew anything they would not admit it.

I forgot to say that before we left the Headman's hut on the second day that the other Burmese hunters made an opium offering to the hunter's God. I guess the God forgot about us but nevertheless it was interesting to watch. They stacked our guns along the palisade that ran around the hut and put the opium in a saucer and a bottle of water beside it and then chanted a few prayers. It was certainly a great trip up into the jungle and I am certainly grateful to Captain Wordinham for giving me the opportunity to go along. The little brown Burmese with their Mongolian features; the smell of the jungle in the air; the little huts in the jungle with the naked children playing g around them; the smell of the Burmese cheroots that our beaters smoked and the fascination of this strange land have all left an impression that I am sure will always remain with me. I have gained respect for the little Burman and his simple way of living; some accuse them of being a lazy people *but perhaps they have merely learned how to really live.* When you climb up the ladder that leads into their hut you may be sure of a welcome and the offer of something to eat and that is more than you can expect from many of these Eastern people. Perhaps we did not break any records in the way of game shot but otherwise it was a perfect trip.

December 5th/38—Moulmein, Burma

I strolled up to the top of Pagoda hill again tonight to watch the sunset, it is certainly a pretty sight. The Salween stretches to the north and separates into several branches in the distance. Far below our ship lay at anchor like a toy ship. The tinkling of the little bells as the breeze sways them in the pagoda tops and the mellow booming of a temple gong in the distance have an attraction all of their own. The occasional Pungency *(Buddhist Monk)* passed by dressed in their orange robes and either carrying one of their large parasols or a begging bowl. The songs of birds in the trees far below came faintly up along with the cries of the children in the streets and the honking of bus horns. It was hard to tear myself away as darkness descended.

December 6th/38—Moulmein, Burma *(Elephants hauling logs)*

Today the 2nd Officer Mr. Sleigh and I visited the teakwood saw mills and watched the elephants at work handling the great logs. It was an amazing sight to see the skill and strength with which these animals do their work. The Indian Mahouts sat on their backs on wooden saddles and they hardly used their little hooked sticks at all to guide their charges. Several of the elephants had long ivory tusks and these were protected by steel guards. They used them for picking up both large piles of various sized scantling and great logs with equal ease.

The noise from the dozens of saws as they ate through the teak logs was certainly terrific. Both Indians and Burmese laborers were employed in the mill which of course was only one of the many mills along the river. We strolled back through the mill to where the logs were being drawn out of the river on a long revolving chain When they were unhooked from the chain at the top a large elephant rolled them over to the saws. The logs were squared off at the first saws then passed on up to other saws to be cut into timbers or scantling or boards as was required. Then the elephants carried it away to the yard where they stacked it up. Sometimes the boards were put on carts that run on rails and the elephants pulled those away as well. Not only did the elephants use tusks and trunks to shift the heavy logs but at times they would use their feet to push them. It was certainly a thrilling sight to see the elephants at work in that teak mill and I hope that common ordinary machinery never replaces them.

December 7th/38—(Moulmein, Burma—The Story of the Golden Pagoda)

This afternoon I went for a walk up past the golden pagoda on the hill. As I stood nearby listening to the tinkling of the temple bells in the afternoon breeze an Indian came along and spoke to me in good English. He insisted on telling me his life history and in the course of our conversation I managed to get the story of the golden pagoda from him as well. It goes as follows:

Several centuries ago the Burmese King and the Siamese King had a quarrel. Now it was the custom in those days for king to fight against king instead of people having to do it all as now a days. I thought this was a very happy idea! Apparently personal combat was equally distasteful to these two kings as well so they decided to build a pagoda each and the one who completed his pagoda first would be the winner.

Of course they called in their people to help with this and the time limit was to be one night and one morning for the completion of the pagoda. In this way they were to decide which King had the most people and who was the most powerful. The Siamese King started to build his upon the site of the Golden Pagoda which is sometimes called the Old Moulmein Pagoda and the Burmese started to build theirs across the river upon a hill.

The Siamese King gathered together his bricks and mortar (the pagodas are solid right through) and was all ready to start building the night before. The Burmese King was quite tricky and decided that he would not risk building one in that way as he would likely be beaten. That night he had a large framework of bamboo set up the same shape as a pagoda. Over this he wrapped sheets of white linen and when completed it looked like a newly completed pagoda. Early the next morning when the Siamese had their pagoda only partly built they looked across the river and saw what looked like a completely built white pagoda. He decided that the Burmese were a very powerful people and fled from Burma with his people. The jubilant Burmese then completed the Siamese King's Pagoda and have a special name for it in Burmese in celebration of their victory.

I followed the road leading past the pagoda down into the town on the other side of the hill and started walking back to the ship through the town. The street was crowded with pedestrians, gharries, motor-buses and bicycles with side cars attached to them. The bus drivers are particularly amusing as no matter how full up they are with Burmese passengers they would willingly dump them all out onto the road and let you climb in if you gave them any encouragement at all. They knew that a white man would pay far more than all his passengers combined and it would pay him to refund their fare. There are no taxis so in that way they act as taxis as well as buses.

December 8th/38—Moulmein Burma

This evening I climbed the hill of the Pagodas once more and watched the sun sink like a ball of orange colored fire in the **west** and a full moon rise out of the **east.** It became much cooler as the sun went down and a slight breeze sprang up starting the little bells tinkling in the cupola of a near-by pagoda. The blue smoke started to rise from the evening fires in the town below and curled up among the palm trees that almost hid the house tops; it must have been mostly teak burning and the smoke smelled very fragrant as it rose to the top of the hill. Several Pungyis passed by, their orange robes making a flare of color along the road. Each Buddhist is expected to send at least one member of the family to train to be a Pungyi and it takes about two years to do so. They shave their heads and go about with their begging bowls from house to house begging for their living. They are allowed no money and must live on what people are willing to give them.

It grew late as I strolled along the top of the hill and it was reluctantly that I descended to the world below again as it was so peaceful up above. We are leaving here tomorrow and will anchor part way down the Salween at Half Way creek and complete our loading there. I wonder if I will ever get back here again? It has certainly been a great stay.

December 14th/38—Calcutta, India. (Tricky Vendors)

We arrived here yesterday and are anchored at Esplanade Moorings just opposite Eden Gardens with it's palm trees and many flowering shrubs. The weather is cool and pleasant here at this time of the year. Have been up town and reported at the B.WM.S. depot today. As usual the streets were filled with chattering Indians. I must say that I much prefer the Burmese to these Indians and if I had to live on shore out East here I would certainly take Burma any day. The chief hobby of these Indians as far as I can see is either begging bakshish from every white man they can see or else trying hard to cheat him when they sell him anything. They use Rupees, Annas and Pice here for coinage and the only way you can be sure that your change isn't counterfeit is to ring all your silver as you get it and examine it closely as well. The shopkeepers often save up their bad silver for just such greenhorns as myself and have already collected several dud Rupees. A Rupee is equal to One shilling and six pence or say about thirty six cents in Canadian currency. Every thing you buy in the bazaars must be examined very closely when you buy it as you can never get your money back if there is anything wrong and when you unwrap it there is almost sure to be something wrong with it if you have not looked at it closely. These people do not seem to worry over whether you will ever go back to their shops again, their one aim in life is to cheat you while you are there.

The Police wear colorful red turbans and sashes with a white uniform. They have puttees wound around their bare legs and wear heavy shoes. They also carry long staffs most of the time. As far as a European is concerned it is useless to ask them for directions as none of them seem to speak any English. You would think that as India is British the police would have to speak a bit of English at least, but apparently that is not so.

December 24th/38—Calcutta, India.

We have been here in Kedderpore Docks for some days now loading coal for Rangoon. Hundreds of Indian men and women are busy carrying baskets of coal up the gangways that lead from the jetty and there is a steady thumping as they toss their loads into the hold. Today is the day before Christmas and tomorrow we will be putting to sea again.

December 25th/38. (Christmas at Sea)

Christmas Day and we are sailing down the Hughli River bound for Rangoon. The Goanese *"boys"* have decorated the saloon up rather nicely for the occasion. They come from Portuguese India around Marmagoa way and are a mixture of Portuguese and Indian blood. They are supposed to be better servants than the Indian Mohammedan *"boys"* and are Catholics so they are quite enthusiastic about Christmas as well. We are not having Christmas dinner until we reach Rangoon so that all can have dinner together. This is certainly not Christmas weather and most unlike Christmas to me.

December 28th/38—At Sea:

We had Christmas dinner today instead of at Rangoon as we first thought. It was certainly good with turkey and all the trimmings and lots of them. All we lacked was a bit of cool weather to give us the proper appetites. Of course it is quite a bit different from having Christmas at home with all the family present but guess we can't have everything.

December 31st/38—Rangoon, Burma

We have been here several days now and we are moored quite far out from shore discharging our cargo of coal. Well this is the last day of old 38 and it has certainly been a great year for me with more traveling done than I ever dreamed about.

Part 3
January 1939

January 1st, 1939—Rangoon

Last night we ushered the New Year in by letting the old whistle do it's stuff and all the other ships in the river did the same and it was a great old racket for a while. This morning all the ships in the river were "dressed" for the occasion and it made a fine sight with all the various flags flying from bow to stern. The flags on all the ships were run up at the same time following the lead of the senior Captain's ship—a British India ship. We had a fine New Year's dinner and as usual on the Indian coast there have been many "burra" kegs of whiskey consumed on board.

January 5th, 1939—" Rangoon, Burma"

Karunakar our Indian Third Officer was shifted today to another ship and we were all sorry to see him go. He came from near Paulghat somewhere in

India on the Malabar Coast and was certainly a real gentleman. I will probably see him again on the coast here sometime.

January 9th/39—Rangoon, Burma

It has been just one year since I left Ontario to come to sea and I have traveled approximately 34,486 miles during this time.

January 14th/39 (Rangoon, Burma)

There has been a lot of rioting lately between the Burmese and the Indians. The Burmese dislike the Indians and don't want them in their county. As there are 1,000,000 Indians in Burma it seems that they have room for complaint. There have been a lot of deaths on both sides and the tension is growing steadily. They expect that there will be fresh rioting next week.

January 21/39 (Rangoon, Burma)

The riots here did not develop as expected and although a few arrests were made it all passed off very quickly. It appears that some Headmen from several jungle villages had journeyed to Rangoon to ask the Government for a reduction in taxes. It is said that the Pungyis (Buddhist Monks) who are proving a rather troublesome lot lately and a few Japanese agitators got among them and started working them up against the Government. The Government heard their case, gave them the requested reduction in taxes and they departed quite happily leaving the Pungyis and the agitators rather holding the bag. We are leaving here tomorrow bound for Bombay, Kathiawar Coast ports and Karachi; all these ports are in India.

January 25th/39—At sea (There she blows)

Today we have been passing along the coast of Ceylon and I saw my first whale since coming to sea. It looked like a wet mass of Indian rubber and kept sending jets of spray into the air—in other words it was "There she blows"!

January 30th, 1939—Bombay, India

We arrived here on the night of the 28th and are anchored far from shore. We have to either catch the launch when it comes out in the morning and return in the evening or else take the native "tonies" which are large dug-out canoes. The tony wallas are mostly a bunch of rogues as they are used to charging the tourists any old price that they wish and think we should pay the same.

February 3rd, 1939—Bhavnagar, India

We arrived here yesterday morning and it is just about as God-forsaken a spot as I have seen. We are tied up alongside a jetty and when the tide goes out we are sitting on the mud bottom. All around us are acres of flat marshy land. The natives make use of the marshy land to collect salt from the sea water and there are gleaming heaps of it in the distance. The town of Bhavnagar has a population of about 75,594 people and half of them probably sleep on the streets if its like most Indian cities. Apparently the land is quite fertile in the interior from what the native supercargo tells me.

February 4th, 1939—Veraval, India

Here we are anchored about a quarter of a mile from shore and unloading into native lighters. The town is made up of white buildings and there seems to be few trees about the place. Within sight is the town of Somnath Patan which is about the same size as Veraval. It has a dark stone wall around it all and within is the ruined temple of Somnath. The temple or the city, I am not sure which, is said to be haunted. Veraval has a population of about 21,114.

Feb. 8th, 1939—Kutch Kundla, India

We are tied up to a jetty here but it is certainly a barren spot. I only see a few native huts near by and not a tree in sight. The main town is apparently several miles away. The natives have built salt pans in the marshes and make salt from the sea water. There are large heaps of salt laying around here which covers anything from an acre to two acres and which are surrounded with mud walls. When they want to fill then they allow the water to run in at high tide and then close the sluice gate. Then the hot sun evaporates the salt water and the Indians merely have to gather up the salt crystals. This is a native state called the state of Kutach and the town is called Kundla. They have their own coinage here and I have taken some as a souvenir. I also managed to get an old East India coin here marked 1840 so feel well pleased with myself.

February 11th, 1939—Karachi, India

Slowly our ship noses its way up the harbor past the silvery Imperial Airway's plane moored at a buoy past sailing dhows with their sails gleaming white in the sunlight, and on past the large City Line steamer with its busy derricks. The tugs skilfully manoeuvre us into our berth alongside the dock. Ropes are made fast ashore, and the tugs depart with a seemingly derisive hoot or two. The gangway is lowered and we are immediately besieged with box wallas, all eager to sell us anything at double it's proper price, or even for a bit less if we really insisted on it. Taxi walla's compete with each other looking for passengers and each one wanders about quoting his license number hoping that someone will remember it. A bearded Sikh sidles up to us, tries hard to assume a mystic expression and wants to tell our fortunes. A snake charmer makes his way on board and puts on his act outside the galley, much to the gratification of our Goanese *"boys"*.

This is a city built on the fringe of the desert and the jumping off place for the North West Frontier. The sandstone buildings are mostly square in shape with flat roofs. The sandhill in the distance breaks the monotony of the scene but does not remove the feeling of the hardness of life in this portion of the world. Tall supercilious looking camels are pulling low rubber tyred carts about the docks. To pull the cart a pad, held in place by a girth, fits just in front of the camel's hump and to this the shaft's of the cart are fastened. As the camels shuffle awkwardly along they often snarl and moan to themselves as though bearing a grudge against the world in general. Other camels kneel patiently between the shafts of their carts, waiting their turn to go alongside the dhows for a load.

Leaving the docks and pausing to look at the freight yards of the North Western Railway we were reminded of the difference between old and new methods of transport as a heavily laden ox cart, pulled by a yoke of oxen, creaked slowly past. As though to draw attention to this difference a loco-motive puffs noisily past the yard entrance. Karachi is the natural port for the province of Sind and the Punjab and it is the most important city in the north western portion of India. The railway of course plays its part in the development of these areas. It serves much of the fertile valley of the river Indus. The Indus is 1,800 miles long with its source in Tibet. It flows through Kashmir, the Punjab, and the province of Sind down into the Arabian Sea. During its periodic floods the river overflows. Here wheat, barley, tobacco and sugar cane are grown and much of it finds its way to Karachi by rail where a good local market prevails as well as an export one. The wheat that is brought in by rail makes up a large part of the seasonal export trade and many steamships and dhows are employed carrying car-goes of wheat to other ports.

The Indians here are a bit different than the southern Indian. They have lighter complexions and are of a sturdier build. There are many hawk nosed Frontiersmen about and their dress is very picturesque. They wear black sleeveless vests that hang quite low and are worn over loose sleeved shirts. The legs of their trousers are quite baggy and they wear leather san-dals with long pointed and upturned toes. Their turbans are wound on stiff forms (probably of glued cloth or leather) and their turban cloth is wound about that; the end of the turban is a broad ribbon that hangs down to their shoulders and it makes them look quite dandified. They always carry something in their hands, either a walking stick or an umbrella. It is said that they are rather fond of walking sticks with long sharp swords in them!

There are also many sturdy looking Sikhs here. They always wear their hair and beards long as that is part of their religion. They usually carry a fancy dagger at their waist which is a reminder that they are decendents of a proud and war-like race. In fact they make up much of the Indian army today.

Here and there one sees a heavily veiled Moslem woman doing some shopping in the bazaars and sometimes a younger and more modern Moslem girl with quite a light veil. From what I have seen though I think that a heavy veil is much preferable for most of them. Some of the women are modern enough around here that they do not wear a veil but they still draw their sari up around the lower part of their face when they see a white man approaching. There are quite a few Arabs as well and of course they are all Moslems.

The people use donkeys and it is amusing to see a wee small donkey pulling a fair sized cart with Abdul perched high up above. They also drive them along with packs on their backs.

It is rather thrilling to see a camel caravan coming in from the desert. First you hear the tinkle of the bells that are hung on the leading camel's neck or perhaps on several of them. Then the first camel sways around a corner followed in turn by many others all carrying huge bales on their backs and one can just imagine the far off outposts on the edge of the desert from whence they come. Even the hay that is used by the animals in the city here has to be imported by camel caravan and of course there is grain, rugs, earthenware, copper ware and many other goods brought in by the same method.

There are many Indian owned gharries around town here and they are always pestering one when you go for a walk. The horses are usually pretty skinny and the way the gharry wallas whip them is shameful. These Indians will not kill any animal, not even to put it out of its misery, but at the same time they are usually very cruel to animals and seem to delight in it.

Many of the pariah dogs that one sees running about are skinny, sore covered wrecks, but no one would kill them.

In the harbor here are many Arab dhows, some from as far away as the Red Sea and others that travel back and forth to Africa. It is amazing the way they get around over such distances. This city (Karachi) is built on one of the smaller deltas of the Indus River. It has a population of about 300,770 people and is about the most important city in this corner of India. There was an Arab invasion here in about 713 A.D. Their rule lasted until 1591 when they were invaded (the country all around here) by the mogul *EMPEROR AKBAR* and then by the *SHAH OF PERSIA* in 1739. The British took charge of this part of the world after the battle of Miani in 1843.

There are many British soldiers about here as regiments are always being relieved up on the North West Frontier—the training ground of the British soldier and a fine looking bunch they are too.

Feb. 13th/39—Karachi, India

I went for a long walk this morning and though pestered to death with gharry wallas I still certainly enjoyed looking around. I'm sure that I would not care to live in this place. I had my camera with me and took a few snaps. The native shopkeepers have the habit of rushing out and wanting you to take snaps of their mangy little shops but I have got wise to that and always tell them that I have just used up the last of my film.

There are many goats and Indian cattle wandering about the streets as in other Indian cities and the streets are not overly clean but are better than in Calcutta. I walked quite a way with a gharry walla driving along behind me until I came to a spot where the gharry wallas descended on me by the dozens. This particular gharry walla had been keeping up a sing-song behind me all the way. He assured me over and over again that he was a poor man; that he *"not charge too much sahib"*, that walking *"not good for white man sahib"*. Anyway his was the nearest gharry when they all swooped down on me so I climbed into it for self protection. It certainly is a Victorian method of getting around but they are still quite in style in these smaller cities. We then bumped along merrily back to our ship.

February 15th, 1939—at sea

Tonight the 3rd Officer called me to see the phosphorus in the water. We seemed to be sailing through a sea of glowing light and along the ships sides the water was a glowing green color. The night was very dark and made the water seem all the more phosphorescent.

February 21st/39 (Pondicherry)

We were at the French port of Pondicherry today for about five hours. The ship was anchored well out from shore and we unloaded into lighters as usual. 2nd Officer Sleigh and I hopped into one of the lighters by crawling down the swaying pilot ladder. As the small boat bobbed about beneath the ladder we had to judge the time to let go and drop the last few feet and at the same time I decided not to crawl down any more swaying rope pilot ladders in the future than was really necessary. We were very high out of the water of course as we only had a few hundred tons of cotton for Pondicherry. We found that the native boat that we had dropped into was built of planks lashed together with fiber; there was a very heavy swell and I began to hope that those lashings were good and strong. We slid up and down the heavy swells as we made the shore and I really enjoyed it. About two hundred feet from shore the insolent natives ceased paddling and began to demand some bakshish. We absolutely refused to give them any as we knew they would demand still more if we gave it to them before they landed us. It was a bit of a stalemate for a while but eventually they landed us and we gave them their bakshish.

We jogged up town in a rickisha and Donald did some shopping and we then went back to the jetty. Every boat walla we went to began demanding a ticket before taking us back to the ship and pointing to the dock office. So we wandered up to it and they told us that we had to pay two Rupees and four annas for a ticket out to the ship.

Apparently the native boatmen got a good rake-off from the ticket because they refused a Rupee to take us back to the ship. We then demanded to see the Port Officer and found him to be a Frenchman who spoke no English. Goodness only knows what the black rascal that did the translating told him but anyway he told us that the Frenchman said we could pay when we reached the ship. That was not the point at all but time was passing so we left and were taken out to the ship. The last I heard as I was going up to my cabin to change was Donald demanding a ticket from the boat walla before we would pay him-tit for tat sort of. Pondicherry is one of the few French possessions in India and it covers an area of about 115 square miles. The Governor in Pondicherry is responsible for the military rule of the other French possessions in India.

Taken from the Karachi Daily (Feb. 13th, 1939)

"Pitched Battles In Cawnpore"—Police Open Fire On Rioters 6 times: 20 killed, 200 Wounded, Scores held. The Police were compelled to open fire on the unruly rioters six times yesterday when several of them were injured. About 300 persons have been arrested for participating in the clashes. More rioters are being rounded every moment. Two Military regiments with fixed bayonets have been stationed in the most badly affected areas. With the break of dawn on Sunday, communal frenzy started near Mulganj area when batches of Hindus and Muslims met in a pitched battle. Lathis, brickbats, knives and other lethal weapons were freely used. "

February 26th/39—Bassein, Burma

Yesterday we came about seventy-five miles up the Bassein River to the town itself; the Bassein River is really a branch of the Irrawaddy and the river boats of the Irrawaddy Flotilla company come here. The town is about the size of Moulmein but without the beautiful scenery. This is in the center of very fertile rice growing districts and we are loading rice from the various mills. The rice mills are scattered along the river here and we will be shifting from one to another to make up our cargo. The land is very flat and ideal for rice (paddy) growing. Coming up the river we picked up the pilot at Diamond Island. We passed jungle clad shore for part of the way up with only a few small hills and of course most of those had a gleaming white pagoda on their summits. The air was filled with the smell of jungle vegetation; a smell that I am sure one would not soon forget as it is so distinctive from other smells. The paddy has just been cut and of course the mills where the husk-covered grain is taken to are all working full time. At the mill the grain is partly cooked to take the husk off and then spread out on the ground to dry. The husk does not actually come off until it goes through another machine that removes it from the rice after it is dried out in the field.

This morning I awoke to a beautiful sunrise and this afternoon I went for a walk along a road filled with many Burmese pedestrians, "rickshaws" and bicycles. There were occasional palm groves and clumps of bamboo along the side and the Burmese women on the other hand enjoy the same rights as the men and can own their own business if they want to.

As I tramped along the dusty road I heard a band getting closer and closer behind me. At length they drew so close that I stepped aside to let them pass by. It turned out to be a Burmese funeral. The band marched in front in great disarray and played for all they were worth. The paper-covered coffin was carried on the shoulders of several men. Several women were walking along with baskets on their heads and no doubt they contained offerings to leave by the side of the grave. Much to my sorrow I had not bothered to take my camera with me and so missed some good snaps.

February 27/1940—Bassein, Burma

The fifth Engineer and I went for a rickshaw ride about the town this afternoon as the ship is now at a paddy mill right near the town and so very convenient for us. We first headed for a huge stone image of Buddha that we could see over the house tops. It looked pretty ancient and there were many temples around it with the ornate wood carved roofs that gradually taper to a spire. They are certainly very picturesque and something that one would not see in any other country. There were many golden and white pagodas inbedded throughout the town.

There are many Burmese craft on the river here. Some of them have sails that remind one of the shell on the Shell gasoline sign, and they look very pretty, especially at sunset when the river is reflecting the red of the sky.

March 1st, 1939—Bassein, Burma

The town looks very pretty from the ship with its pagodas, its palm trees and the white Indian mosque with its minarets. Along the waterfront roadway I can see dozens of rickshaws speeding along and hear the mournful honking of the buses. All the buses and cars in India and Burma use bulb horns that you have to squeeze; the result is a low and mournful honk that is much like a cow mooing.

March 2nd/39—Bassein, Burma—the other day a small Burmese boy

was drowned in the river here and tonight the Kurrani (ships clerk) pointed out a mattress floating on the river with a lighted candle on it. He told me that the Burmese believe that the boy's body will be brought to the surface of the river with this method.

Snipe Hunting

March 3rd/39—Bassein, Burma (Snipe Hunting)

This morning Captain Wordingham asked me if I would care to go snipe shooting with him in the afternoon and of course the answer was "yes"! We left about 1:30 PM with an Indian whose father owned the car and a Burmese hunter to show us the way. We drove out into the country and walked for about an hour before reaching the snipe shooting grounds. The sun was blazing hot and the paddy fields that we had to walk over were certainly rough as they allow the cattle on them when they are still partly flooded. We tramped and and climbed over the paddy fields (they are quite low) and at last reached our starting point. I had little idea of what snipe shooting was and was rather surprised to find that we had to walk through flooded paddy fields to scare up the snipe. The mud was up over our ankles and at times it was almost knee deep and I was glad that I had worn shorts.

There were snipe there right enough but I was too busy trying to keep from sitting down in the mud most of the time to be much of a success at it. The Captain in his element and brought down quite a few snipe. I had a feeling that there would likely be snakes in places like that and so it suited me fine when they suggested we try jungle fowl shooting along towards evening. It was nice standing beside the jungle and letting the beaters do all the work for a change; also with the sun getting a bit lower it was cooler. There is a certain fascination about standing by a jungle trail or beside a jungle clearing and hearing the shouts of the beaters as they draw near you. It is a fascination that is hard to explain. We only shot a couple of jungle fowl but those with the snipe that Captain had shot made a very fair afternoon's bag. It was almost dark by the time we reached our car again and the sun had set before we reached the town. I certainly owe Captain Wordingham a lot for the chances he has given me to look around here in Burma.

March 4ᵗʰ, 1939

We are sailing down the river to the sea in easy stages anchoring every so often to wait for the right tides to get us over the various sand bars. We are bound for Rangoon to complete loading.

March 5ᵗʰ/39—Rangoon, Burma

We arrived here this afternoon and as usual we are moored well out in the river and must get ashore by sampan. It is about 95 degrees F. in the shade most of the day but not too bad at night.

March 22/39—Bombay, India

The ship is now alongside a dock and I reported at the B.W.M.S. Depot today. This afternoon when I got through at the depot I met 2ⁿᵈ Officer Kew and we wandered about the city. It is a very confusing city to find your way about and we managed to get a bit lost once or twice.

March 24th/39—Bombay, India

We shifted out into the bay again today and we are sailing for Quilon, India. This is the place that is famous for its Kashmir nuts and most of them are shipped to America. Strangely enough we are unloading bags of them here from Kenya, South Africa. They came via Bombay where we picked them up. They will be shelled here and prepared for their trip to America.

March 28th/39—Quilon, India

We are now loading the boxes of prepared Kashmir nuts for Colombo, Ceylon where they will be transshipped. We will not be going to Tuticorin after all as orders have changed. Our next port is Colombo, Ceylon. We will leave tonight.

March 30th/39—Akyab, Burma

We are anchored about half a mile from shore and will be loading rice. The only way to get ashore is by sampan. There are many palm trees around the town and native palm thatched huts and temples and pagodas make up the scenery. The weather is pretty hot and I sure have prickly heat.

April 5th/39—Akyab, Burma

I went ashore today via sampan to get some dope from the doctor for my prickly heat rashes. The town is pretty ramshackle when you get into it and not as attractive as when seen from the ship. This place is near the Indian border so there are many Indians here as well as Burmese. It was even hotter ashore than on the ship and I am glad that I do not have to live here.

April 11th/39—Calcutta, India

I reported at B.W.M.S. Depot today and afterwards we went to the pictures with another Radio Officer that I met at the depot. The picture houses are mostly air conditioned here fortunately and one can cool off a bit in them. It is certainly scorching hot here this time of year. It is around 106 degrees in the shade these days and the moment one moves from under a fan why ones shirt is dripping with perspiration. This afternoon I went up town in time to have a bang-up tiffin at the Great Eastern Hotel and then I met Captain Wordingham at the Calcutta Swimming Club. It is quite an exclusive spot and of course I saw more Europeans there than I had seen for a long time.

April 29th/39—Rangoon

2nd Officer Kew and I were ashore all afternoon to get away from the coal dust as it is being unloaded now. He has bought a camera from the 5th Engineer Moody so now I have company in my search for snaps. We had just stepped ashore from our sampan and were walking up the street when we heard a bang of a noise coming down one of the side streets so we investigated. It was a procession that was about a block long and apparently it was either a Chinese wedding or else a funeral, its pretty hard to tell just which in the East. There are a lot of Chinese in Rangoon and they must make up at least a quarter of its population. At the head of the procession were a lot of Chinamen beating cymbals and gongs and making a great old racket. They were probably doing that to scare the evil spirits away. Then we saw what looked to be a coffin on a truck so we decided that it must be a funeral instead of a wedding. It was covered with bright red paper and the truck was well decorated. After the truck followed a band on foot and they were playing away in great style. The truck with the coffin on it was being pulled along the road by means of ropes. After the band followed Chinese Buddhist priests and many other Chinese, both on foot and riding in rickshaws.

We wandered through all the markets with their sights, sounds, smells and colors, through vegetable markets, cloth markets, etc. After having a game of billiards at the Marine Club we returned to the *Indora*. On the way back we passed an Albino Indian. His skin was very pale and rather pinkish and he certainly looked queer. I understand there are quite a number of such Indians and it is merely caused through lack of some pigment in the skin.

Rangoon is a very cosmopolitan place with only a small proportion of Burmese in it. The rest are either Chinese or Indian. The Chinese section is always rather interesting despite the various smells one encounters. The Chinese are very neat and clean compared to the Indians we usually encounter. The Burmese have a very great dislike of the Indians and that has been the cause of a lot of rioting here. Most of the landowners, moneylenders, etc. are Indians and that is part of the trouble I think.

May 1st, 1939—Shwe Dagon Pagoda, Rangoon

I had quite an interesting day ashore with the 2nd today. We visited the Shwe Dagon Pagoda again. The Shwe Dagon is two-hundred and some odd feet high, studded at the top with precious jewels and is covered with golf-leaf. It is the largest and most famous pagoda in the world. It is built at the top of a hill and is reached by four covered staircases which lead up to the walled yard surrounding the Pagoda. This space around the Pagoda covers several acres and is covered with temples which contain many well carved budha idols, etc. The Shwe Dagon pagoda itself is surrounded by many small golden pagodas with a broad marble roadway around it and the above mentioned temples outside this. There is a bell weighing forty eight tons and many smaller ones. Glass tinkles against the top of this Pagoda in the breeze, the glass being suspended by string from the fret-work like ridge several feet down from the top of each Pagoda. Some of the Burmese woodwork on the roof of many of the temples is really marvelous and gives them the real eastern touch.

The sun was very hot and did we ever suffer in our bare feet on the pavement around the pagoda. We took a lot of snaps but I think I had the lens of my camera in backwards so they may not turn out. It was nice to see it again and I think I saw far more than on my first visit. I must say that being barefooted rather cramps a person's style and hopping about as though you were on a frying pan might not be everyone's idea of pleasure. At any rate it was fairly cool in the temples and in their shade. When we returned to the ship we bathed our feet in strong disinfectant just to make sure there were no Indian or Burmese germs hanging about but I am sure they would be well fried anyway—boy are my feet ever sore tonight and old Kew is limping as well.

May 2nd, 1939—Rangoon

I collected snaps taken yesterday when ashore this afternoon and I did have my camera lens in the wrong way. How very annoying after nearly roasting my feet off to get those snaps!!!!!!!!!!!!!!

May 14th/39: (Monsoons and Mangosteens)

Today is Sunday but the cargo work never stops on the Indian Coast. The North-West monsoons are really breaking now and the rain comes down in bucketfuls at times. The hot air is so humid that our shoes and blue suits become covered with mold if not brushed daily—anyway the *"boy"* has to do it so I shouldn't worry. This climate makes one rather languid and I can begin to realize how some men can resign themselves to years on the coast here. Even now I sometimes feel as though any other life that I have known is ages away. The letters from home are about the only real link for me with another world. The start of the rainy season has brought out millions of flying insects and they cluster about our lights at night There are huge crickets, grasshoppers, mosquitoes and large Bombay cockroaches for a start and some of the others can bite like the mischief.

Lately we have been getting some new kinds of fruit for our afternoon tea. It is the first time that I have tasted mangoes and I am sure that I will become very fond of them if we have many. They have a yellow skin and the fruit is very delicious. They taste something like a mixture of peaches, grapes and plums. The pit is similar to a large peach stone and the fruit clings to it. Then there are mangosteens as well and they are better still. The blue rind breaks away from the fruit very easily and the white luscious fruit is in separate sections around the soft seeds. The outside of the mangosteen is really a brownish color but the thick rind is more of a blue or purplish color and very juicy. They are about the nicest fruit I have ever tasted.

May 15th, 1939

To our regret Captain Wordingham has been shifted to another vessel. I can truly say that he is about the best skipper I have sailed with to date. I shall always remember with pleasure our hunting trips together, particularly the several days hunting we had in the Burmese jungles from Moulmein. He has left his fine large Phillip's radio with me until we meet in some other port as he didn't want to take it through the customs here. Now we have plenty of music. The new Captain joined ship today but I haven't met him yet. We are sailing tomorrow morning for Bombay and we expect rough weather with North-West monsoons. It has been raining hard all day and has cooled things off a lot.

May 29th/39—Bombay, India

Here we are again at the Gateway of India. The actual gateway itself, which is near the Taj Hotel, can be seen very clearly from where we are anchored. Unfortunately they only left us in dock one day and then shifted us back into the bay so it is very awkward getting ashore. The usual means of conveyance are very large deep dugouts called "tonies" and they use a sail when the breeze is favorable.

Bombay is very clean and quiet compared with Calcutta. The natives here are also a different type. The cargo workers here are mostly Pathans and are certainly a sturdy looking bunch. They come from dry desert country and it is amusing to see them drinking. They carefully pour out the water from their jugs into a tin, then if there is any water left they carefully pour it back into their jugs even though it is plentiful here. The careful habits formed on the desert are hard to break. It is very beautiful here in the bay and much cooler than Calcutta and Rangoon. We are sailing for the Gulf of Kutch ports and Karachi tomorrow.

Part 4
War

○ ○

Come, fill the Cup, and in the
Fire of Spring
The Winter Garment of Re-
pentance fling:
The Bird of Time has but
a little way
To fly-and lo! The Bird is
on the wing.

(Rubaiyat of Omar Khayyam)

June 2nd, 1939—Bhavnagar, India.

Here we are at one of the native state ports on the Gulf of Kutch in the north-west portion of India. We are tied up at a jetty and at low tide the ship rests on the soft mud out of which the port was scooped. The tide rises from low tide up to thirty one feet higher at high tide. Part of the time we are high above the jetty and at low tide far below it. Around us stretches miles and miles of desolate salt marshes and the town itself can just be seen eight miles away. This is the second time I have had the misfortune to come to this place on the *Indora*.

June 3rd, 1939—Last night there was a full moon so the 3rd and I decided

to go for a walk ashore and on our way we met the clerk and persuaded him to come along. We walked and walked until we came to the town itself which was eight miles away! We wandered about the town, managed to find a place to buy sodas and then we walked back. I must say that a soda is pretty flat stuff without the other half! Anyway as we drank it we had quite an audience of open mouthed staring natives as they watched us through the open front of the shop. They don't usually see white men in this place. All this while a radio that they had in the shop was (Indian fashion) turned on full strength and was shrieking, wailing and fairly spitting Indian music at us until we nearly shrieked as well for them to shut it off! Thus fortified with the potent soda we wandered about the streets. Some of the domed buildings built in the style of the orient were quite beautiful as they lay bathed in the silent moonlight of the night.

At length we passed along out of the town back over the desert road and the eight long weary miles back to the ship. With the land being perfectly flat nothing seems very far away. We thought we would perish of thirst the last five miles back and am I ever stiff today!

June 6th/39: Bedi Bundar, India

This is another hopeless spot as we are anchored about two miles from shore. We arrived here yesterday and are leaving here tonight—thank goodness. Anyway I keep part watches in these spots as they have small radio stations along the shore that are always calling up for the agents and cargo people so it helps to pass the time away. We are going to Navlaki next which is about 35 miles away.

June 10th/39—Karachi, India

We arrived here this morning and as soon as the gangway was lowered we were fairly besieged by the usual mob of Indian box-wallas, tailors and fortune tellers. Even the taxi-wallas come on board here and try to get you to promise to take their taxi when you go ashore. They wander about repeating their taxi license numbers like a bunch of parrots in the hope that you will remember it. One very black taxi-walla with a very wide grin informed me that his name was Bill and this afternoon when the 2nd and I went up to Keamari to do some shopping he was overjoyed when I remembered his name. Keamari is the small town that has grown up around the docks here and used to thrive a lot on the tourist trade and has many curio shops in it. Karachi is a bit further away.

June 11th/39—Karachi (Fishing expedition)

Last night a bunch of us hired an Indian dhow and went out fishing. It was manned by an Indian named Abdul and several others. We went early in the evening and took a goodly lunch and plenty of liquid refreshment. We sailed along at a pretty good clip until we reached the fishing grounds just off Keamari Point and then we anchored. There was quite a breeze blowing and a fair swell and we certainly rolled a lot at anchor. Fishing lines were produced and baited by the Indians for us with prawns and they both smelled pretty strong. The fish were certainly biting good and we started hauling them in right away. The Dhow had a peculiar lurching roll and it was not long before the 4th Engineer was laying in the bottom and wishing he could die in a speedy manner and not like that. That is he was laying in the bottom when he was not leaning over the side casting ground bait to the fishes. I had missed my tiffin and so sampled some of the curry puffs that Ginger Street had bought us as we fished but it was not so long before I had cause to hate the thought of curry puffs. I caught an extra strong whiff of those fishy lines and hastily leaned over the side.

The mate thought I had caught another fish and excitedly asked if it was a big one. "Yes", I replied as sarcastically as I could under the circumstances" "Just watch for it" and then I continued to feed the fishes. However it was just a passing twinge and I was soon as well as ever and caught quite a few fish. The poor 4th was out the whole time though and merely groaned when we spoke to him. Some of the others began to feel a bit shaky with the lurching of the dhow so we pulled up anchor and Abdul sailed her into calmer water where we continued fishing. Our luck petered out but I managed to catch a huge crab. In the excitement I nearly dropped it on the neck of the poor 4th who was now asleep from sheer exhaustion now that we were in smoother water. Next I nearly dropped it on the mate who was fishing beside me and then it fell off the hook and Adam (the boy) grabbed it. All this time it was dark and we only had a lantern to see by aboard the dhow. I couldn't make out what the darned thing was as it clattered on board. The mate is a cheerful bloke and all the while he kept up a running chatter and kept the party alive. The poor 4th managed to groan out "I don't know how you blokes can be so happy", just before he fell asleep.

We arrived back about midnight and the 4th's first action on reaching land was to lay down on the grass, stretch out his arms and murmur "good old terra firma". This morning at breakfast the Captain greeted me with "I hear you're a fine bunch of sailors!" Which I rather sheepishly admitted was quite true. "Well", he added, "I can stand a naval destroyer's roll or any ship going in rough water but I still get sick in one of these dhows when its anchored in rough weather!" Apparently it is all in what you are used to. We caught about seventy-five fish last night. The largest was about three feet long.

June 12th/39—Karachi, India

I went for a good long walk this morning and took quite a few snaps. It is always interesting to see the camels pulling their carts or to see a camel caravan swaying through the streets. The camel is a very surly beast though and would as soon bite you as look at you if he had the chance. They are always grumbling and groaning to themselves in a very dissatisfied way and seem to have a grudge against the world. They have the queerest swaying motion that I have seen as they trot or walk along. I would like a ride on one but their motion reminds me of that dhow the other night and this is much too soon after that experience. We are leaving here tomorrow bound for Moulmein, Burma once more and I am looking forward to seeing it again.

June 15th/39—at sea

We are having heavy weather as this is monsoon time. The ship is light and we are rolling a lot. Everything movable seems to be on the deck of my cabin.

June 19th, 1939: S.S. Indora in the Bay of Bengal

Position 8.5 Long 85.59F.—bound for Moulmein at 0048. Picked up call from GTOB the S.S. Deebank Lat 15.32 N. Long 92.86E lost propeller requires assistance please give positions of offering—master
However there were ships closer at hand than we were and at 0144 GMT I picked up the following message from Deebank-CQ—thanks for positions and messages have now arranged assistance—Master.

June 21st/39—At sea

We are having a rough trip as the monsoon never seems to let up. It pours rain part of the time and there is usually a gale blowing.

June 23rd/39—Moulmein, Burma

We arrived here yesterday afternoon and the rain continues to pour down in proper tropical style. This town still looked as inviting as ever from where we were anchored in the Sabween river and the gleaming pagoda's on the hill still held a most fascinating interest for me.

On Saturday the 2nd Officer and I visited the teak mills and watched the elephants work. In Moulmein there are about four means of conveyance. You can ride in a garry or in a bicycle with a boat shaped side car attached in which two can sit. However one must sit facing forward with knees bent up and the other must sit facing aft with their back against the chap in front. Feet must dangle or rest over the step below. You can also take the occasional rickshaw or best of all there is the bus!

These buses are mostly old Ford or Chevy cars, etc. The drivers drive "like a bat out of hell"! As you walk along the street the bus drivers with their loads of passengers invariably spot you. *"Where to Sahib"* he shouts and if you want to hire him for two or three rupees for the afternoon he promptly chucks all of his passengers out on the road, refunds their few coins and in you climb. The passengers have to find another bus but they seem to accept this practice with the stoicism of the east. The place seems to be full of buses and every last bus driver either slows down or stops and tries to persuade you to hire the bus.

The garry walla is of course an ever present nuisance in any of these small Burmese or Indian ports. With his little horse, his bundle of hay for the noonday feed on the seat beside him and the garry walla himself perched on top of the garry in proper old stage coach style. This is something you cannot see in any other port of the world.

June 24th/39—Moulmein (Elephant riding)

Today it slacked off raining a bit and Kew the 2nd Officer and I visited the teak mills again and watched the elephants at work and took some more snaps. Here there were about a dozen elephants hard at work and the whine of countless saws filled the air. We watched the elephants with great admiration. It is certainly marvelous the way they can pick up anything from a small scantling to a huge teak timber. Some of the elephants must have weighed at least 5 tons. They picked up timber with their trunks and pushed the timber with their front feet. Under the guidance of their mahouts they seemed capable of doing most anything. Long may they survive the machine age! The mahouts, with the idea of obtaining a little bakshish, willingly made the elephants pose while we took snaps.

One of the mahouts asked us if we wanted a ride on his elephant and I was all for getting Kew to take a ride. I even offered to take a snap of him on the elephant to show his future grandchildren but he was most ungrateful and stubborn and suggested that I go up myself—so I did but with rather a few misgivings. The mahout made the elephant kneel down which it did with a few protesting groans and trumpetings and then up got the elephant with a clumsy, rocking, swaying motion while I clung to the wooden cross trees of the saddle for dear life! I had given the 2nd my camera to take some snaps while I was up to such great heights and I hope they turn out okay. The elephant went on piling teak and as I sat up there with the mahout I began to realize why the Rajahs of India always chose elephants for their parades and ceremonies. They certainly are powerful brutes and it was great to watch the way this elephant handled the heavy timbers as well as the bundles of teak scant ling. I was filled with pity for poor old Kew—the 2nd who was a mere man on the ground!

On dismounting Kew decided he wouldn't mind trying it as well but we had used up all our camera film so decided to go back another day.

June 26/39

We left the ship after breakfast and climbed to the top of the hill overlooking Moulmein. We wandered along the roadway that winds along the top of the hill. We enjoyed the panorama stretched out on all sides below us as well as the pagodas on the hill itself. Miles on both sides were flooded paddy fields. The river was broad and placid looking from that height and stretched as far as eyes could see to the north-west while another branch wound around a high hill and wound northeastward toward China. These rivers are a regular net work of inland waterways. Hills, looking as though a careless maker had dropped them clear out of the sky into the paddy fields, dotted the landscape.

From below we could here the singing of a Burmese choir in a Christian church below and as we set near the base of Kipling's pagoda and discussed his 'R*oad to Mandalay*" the world of automobiles, airplanes, rush, fear and worry seemed far away. Only our ship swinging at anchor far below reminded us of the year 1939. The town itself could hardly be seen below on account of its tropical foliage of palms of various kinds. Large long Burmese dugout canoes with their bamboo mats and sunshades and other craft with their queer sails could be seen sailing up and down the river. It was indeed a beautiful panorama.

Descending the hill via the stairway leading to one of the pagodas we wandered along the main street. Happening to spy an opening into what appeared to be a cloth market we went in and upon passing piles and piles of gaily colored cloth found it opened up still further into building after building of market produce. It extended all along the water front so that the queer shaped Burmese river craft could empty their market wares directly into the market.

We examined the skillfully made bark hats that we saw so many of the boatmen wear. The cheerful, smiling Burman selling these hats knew a little English and he told us that they were made of bamboo bark and were quite waterproof. The sharp pointed top is tipped with tin. They only cost five annas each and if they were not so large I would have liked to have bought one as a souvenir. We discovered all sorts of strange corners in the market each stuffed with produce which made us wonder how many years it would take to sell it all! We priced a soapstone Buddha and the vendor asked the exorbitant price of three Rupees and in true oriental fashion called after us as we departed: *"How much you give, how much you give"* but we were deaf!

We asked the prices of the multitude of various sized cheroots from a smiling Burmese girl who knew no English but who gigglingly proceeded to teach us the Burmese names of the Cheroots. We held our noses through the fish and meat markets, inspected the gay and varied assortment of tropical fruits in the fruit section, wandered through the pottery portion, on through the clothing, tinware and tinsmith part and soon out into the street again.

June 30th/39—Moulmein

The 5th Engineer and I went to the teak saw mill again and watched the elephants at work. It is certainly worth several visits and as there is always the chance that I will not be back again so it is best to make the most of my opportunities. Rookerman's Saw mill is the handiest for us (it is an Indian word but we pronounce it that way) although there are many others along the river. From where we are moored in the river we can hear the whine of the saws in the teak mills.

July 1st/39—Moulmein, Burma (Practical Jokes)

This morning when I was still sleeping the 3rd brought up a new kind of fruit and shoved it under my mosquito net. It was horrible smelling fruit and I immediately begged that gentleman to kindly remove self and fruit from my cabin … it smelled like a combination of cheese factory, sewer gas and a skunk at close quarters. It is called Durian fruit here and is greatly prized by the Burmese and other Eastern people who claim it has wonderful aphrodisiac powers. It has a rough russet skin or peel and the white meat is wound about the seeds inside. It had a rather sickening taste and I didn't like it at all. The smell of the broken skin—wow-it would move anything but an Easterner. This afternoon I had a brilliant idea. Rushing below I enlightened the suddenly delighted 3rd with my plan. The boy was called upon to produce the empty husks of the dorraine, which when broken smelled twice as bad and we gently opened the 2nd's door and I silently and lovingly placed that horrible smelling husk beside the head of his bunk. Outside his cabin we could smell the stuff even through the walls! It was a great success as he had all manner of bad dreams with bad smells playing a great part in them. At length he awoke and discovered the durian peels and a smell in his cabin that would make the dead hold their noses. So now I think I have repaid him for several practical jokes! However I had better beware for a while, he swears that he will find some horrible revenge or other.

That afternoon I had some of the fruit which is a white slimy sort of stuff wrapped in folds about the seeds which are quite large and like nuts. I didn't like it at all. The outside husk is greenish in color and very sharp points are all over it. It is about the same size as an ordinary pineapple and is one of the Burman's most treasured fruits. They are welcome to them!

July 2nd/39—Moulmein (A posh Affair)

Most of us went to the annual ball of the local Battalion here. It is called the Tenasserim Battalion and it was fairly good turn-out. They had dancing and served weak whiskey and ended up with a free lunch. We all wore mess kits the same as the Army officers and the civilians who were present wore their dinner suits and tails and all told it was quite a posh affair. Even on the outposts of the Empire they manage to have good military flings. The men mostly wore dinner suits(tux) and the white civilians wore tails. Without saying it in a conceited way I think that the ship's officers from our own and one other British ship in port were the smartest appearing of the lot. We arrived back this morning about dawn and I brought the Clerk back with me and pushed him up the gangway and helped him to his cabin for he had indulged well if not wisely despite weak whiskey. Tomorrow we are proceeding to Rangoon to complete our cargo.

July 13th/39 (Rescue at sea)

I saw my first rescue at sea today. While at breakfast in the saloon the 3rd Officer reported a country (native) boat in distress on the port side. As we drew near we could see that boat was only about 35 feet long and all available space filled with people. We got quite close from this side but the inmates of the boat appeared too weak to paddle any closer to us and the boat drifted away. The Captain put ship full astern and then approached with the boat on the starboard side giving it some protection from the heavy seas. That native boat, lashed together with thongs, rode those huge waves and was indeed marvelous to behold. One moment it would be entirely hidden from sight behind a wave except for mast a then it would slide up the waves and at a perilous angle slip down the other side. I have heard that these native craft are almost unsinkable and now I believe it. Coming alongside we could see a pitiful mass of humanity down below. Without a doubt they were just about at the end of their endurance. Before lines could be secured, it came up against that ship's side with a couple of nasty wallops which apparently spelled its end, for it sank immediately as we started on our way again.

The pilot ladder was lowered into the boat which was bobbing down below. Lines were passed around the waists of the weaker ones and in that way assisted up the pilot. Fortunately we are heavily loaded so not up too high out of the water. All were helped out of the boat in this manner except one and what a pitiful sight he was, even looking at him from above. Obviously a cripple, he was now nothing but a bundle of bones held together with skin. I have never seen such a horrible sight. A canvas with ropes at each of the four corners was lowered and a kalasi (sailor) rolled him into it and he was pulled up.

All of the boat's inmates were men and every one was too weak to stand as they came on deck. Their hands and feet were bleached white from salt water and their bodies covered with salt water sores. No one could understand them at first until we found out that one of them spoke a bit of Hindustani but first they were given some water, precious water and then a little food—but only a little at first owing to the ill-effects of too much after starvation.

We watched the curious shaped boat with its queer curved paddles drop away behind us then slowly settle down to the bottom of Davy Jones locker. It appears they had been caught in a storm while crossing from the Maldive Islands to the Laccadive Islands, a six hour run. These islands are south-west of Ceylon and we were north of the Andaman Islands in the bay of Bengal. The exact distance was a bit over 1300 miles! Just think of it—over 1300 miles in a small 35 foot boat with twelve inmates in it, no food and only brackish rain water which the rains provided to drink. They had been drifting for thirty days, one man had died the twelfth day out and had been thrown overboard. The more I think of being thirty days at sea and traveling over 1300 miles in that cockle-shell of a boat the more I marvel at it. It is certainly wonderful what men can endure. Today all all are up except the cripple. We will take them on around to Bombay with us.

July 23rd/39—Bombay, India

We arrived here on the 21st and have been in the Alexandra Dock ever since which is very handy. Today is Sunday and this morning Kew, Burroughs and myself hired some bicycles and spent the day wandering about the city at our leisure. First we cycled along the sea front and then up the Malabar Hill where stand the Parsi *"Towers of Silence"* where the Parsis put their dead. The bodies are lain on gratings on top of the towers and the vultures, crows and kites do the rest. The bones drop down through the gratings into a well underneath from what I hear. We could not go inside but I'm not very keen on seeing dead bodies at any time. The place was well surrounded by trees so there is not much to see from outside but from the hill itself we had a marvelous view down over the city and the bay. Coasting down the hill we passed through another portion of the city and out among some more hills and at the top of one of them we saw a fakir's flag flying. We decided to have a look at the old boy so leaving our bicycles at the foot of the hill we climbed up it. We found the habitat of this person to consist of mud walls with a roof of cotton to keep the sun out! I didn't find out what he did when it rained. To our surprise he also had a wife and a brood of naked, dirty children. He had an altar built at the head of the steps and it looked much like an old clay oven. He smeared some bright yellow powder and then some red powder over his forehead and did the same to one of the junior fakirs and then tried hard to look mystic as he yanked on a couple of cow bells. Apparently this hill had acquired great merit among the Indian matrons as a once barren matron had came here and prayed for a son and she then had one. Ever since that day the hill had been a tearing success and the fakir has apparently done a thriving business. After looking at the Fakir's large brood of children I thought I could offer a more reasonable explanation as to the reason the visiting Indian ladies had children. We gave the fakir a few annas bakshish and left with the old boy in full cry behind us after more bakshish. He almost got a kick in the nether regions for his pains.

Next we visited the zoo where the keepers small son spotted us and wanted to show us the baby lion cubs for some bakshish. He led us through the crowd of Indians that wanted to get in to see them as well and when they asked why they could not get in as well why he told them we were doctors—so there we were trying to look like doctors as we strode along …

We drove back through the bazaar section and the streets were crowded with Indians, ox carts, holy cattle, etc. and all the color and the smells of the east. I'm a bit stiff tonight but it has been a very successful day.

August 12th/39—Madras, India

We rushed around here to Madras to take general cargo to Rangoon. Owing to so many of the regular British India Ships being called in by the government to be used for troopships it has interrupted the regular services. Here we are after a rough trip around and plenty of rolling done. I was up town this afternoon and I think this is about the dirtiest city I have seen in India up to date and that is saying quite a bit. There are some fine buildings but there are natives living around them in small dirty burlap tents and on the open ground, talk about squalor. Everywhere there are beggars—both male, female and children. Of course there are the usual pesky rickisha wallas and so called guides. The High Court here is a marvelous building with oriental spires and a light as in a lighthouse combined with one of them. The building itself is of red brick on the wall surrounding the high Court are several brass plates telling that as these spots shells landed and bursts that were fired from German cruiser Emesden during the great war.

There are a lot of marvelously carved Hindu temples about here and they have all sorts of figures carved on them. There is one that we can see from the ship here that looks like a huge head in the distance *(after the Egyptian sphinx fashion)* but close up it is row after row of stone images around it. Each little statuette on the temple itself is very complete and as I looked at the dirty smelly rabble passing below I marveled at the fact that it was their work. The various statues each represented something of course and I recognized several Hindu Gods.

August 19th/39—Rangoon, Burma

We arrived here on the 17th and we are now moored way out in the river. It has been raining steady and the river is flooding making it rather dangerous to try and get ashore. There are tons and tons of water hyacinths floating down the river just now. They have broken loose from up-river where they are a nuisance to navigation and they are full of water snakes and scorpions. The hyacinths sometimes cling to the teak timbers here as they are lifted out of the water and the cargo coolies sometimes get bitten by the snakes or scorpions. These flood waters are so strong in the river at times that the steam tugs can hardly go against it. Some of the streets are flooding at high tide in the city now. I wonder if it will ever stop raining.

August 22/1939 (Risk of TB on the S/S Sir Harvey Adamson)

I was transferred to here in a HURRY this afternoon. A launch came out to where the *Indora* is moored for me and with just enough clothing for the trip to Mergui and back I came to this ship. I am to rejoin the *Indora* when we get back in a few days as she will still be loading teak and rice here. This is a small ship built years ago for this run. She is only a little over a thousand tons and carries passengers and some freight. The chap I am relieving for this trip is in hospital just now; they tell me he suffers from T.B. I can't say I like the idea of moving right into his cabin in such a hot damp, climate as this but nothing much I can do about it really.

August 23rd/39—S/S Sir Harvey Adamson

We moored in the river about nine miles down from Tavoy and unloaded into barges. Then on to Mergui here which we reached late tonight. The scenery has been wonderful all along the coast here; it is rugged jungle and the air is fragrant with that peculiar fragrant smell of wood smoke and jungle that seems to be so much a part of Burma. All we can see of Mergui tonight is the pagoda on the hill that is rimmed with lights and a few lights ranging along the base of the hill.

As soon as we were moored, or rather anchored, in the bay here a great swarm of sampans came swooping down on the tide and all tried to make the gangway at once. They had come off to meet the many passengers that we carried and there was true oriental confusion as they swarmed around the foot of the gangway. It ended with a couple of Chinamen tumbling into the briny and being well ducked and carried along with the tide in the darkness before they were finally rescued. Then they swooped down to the gangway one after the other in a more orderly manner.

August 24th/1939 S/S Sir Harvey Adamson

The countryside is really beautiful here with rugged jungle-covered hills and many small islands along the coast. This afternoon the 4th Engineer and I went for a walk ashore. It rained constantly though we did not mind that as much as we did that it prevented us taking snapshots. We wandered up past the pagoda on the hill where we could hear the little bells tinkling and went on out amongst the rubber plantations and the palm groves on the outskirts of the little town. There were also many clumps of feathery looking bamboo. It was my first close-up of rubber trees and I was interested to see how they had been tapped though there were none that were actually being tapped at the time. The town itself is pretty much on the jungle side as might be expected and in no way detracts from its charm. The inhabitants are a mixture of Burmese, Siamese and Chinese. Besides exporting rubber and tin from here the natives do very fine work in carving mother-of-pearl.

Part of our return cargo from here consists of "napee". It is a very pure mixture of very rotten fish that has been buried in the ground for several weeks and allowed to decompose. This is considered a great delicacy by the Burmese, hence our very odoriferous cargo; and certainly it does smell to high heaven. Possibly it is a good thing that it is monsoon time on the Bay, might blow a bit of the smell away.

August 27th, 1939—S/S Indora

Rejoined the *Indora* today from the *Sir Harvey Adamson*. A launch brought me back here as soon as we arrived this morning. It rained steadily for almost the whole of that trip and continues to do so. Everything is damp and soggy, clothes and shoes soon become green with mildew here unless brushed often. It is rather nice to get back here again despite the fact that there was a good crowd on the *Sir Harvey*. For one thing she has a devilish sideways roll in the heavy monsoon seas and I did not feel any too happy about it at times. There was quite a difference from the steady roll of the much larger *Indora*. *It looks as though we will soon be at war now though we all hope that by some miracle it might be avoided. We are already under Admiralty control. Most of us would hate to see Britain back down from the demands being made by Germany.*

August 30th/39—S/S Indora—(Looming War)

We are at sea again bound for Bombay-Kathiawar-Karachi ports with our usual cargo of teak lumber and rice. Things look pretty bad just now and we may be at war with Germany at any moment. That is not a very happy thought and we all hope that it may be avoided by some last moment miracle. We are traveling in complete darkness at night now "just in case" and have orders not to use the wireless transmitter unless specially ordered to do so.

August 31, 1939—S/S Indora

Quite a monsoon blowing just now. At present the air seems strangely silent with no British ships using wireless; I hope that this is another false alarm and that things may soon get back to normal. *These are certainly strange and unsettled days that we have the misfortune to live in.*

September 1st, 1939—S.S. Indora: *(Tension)*

The monsoon has eased off a bit in the Bay of Bengal here and it is much pleasanter now. We all wait resignedly to learn if it will be peace or war. *With the wireless silence in force I can almost feel the tenseness in the air itself. Rather looks as though Chamberlain and his umbrella can do little to avoid war this time. Anyway it has been coming for a long time now, best to get it over with perhaps.*

September 2nd, 1939—S.S./Indora

We are rolling along across the Bay of Bengal. The air certainly seems silent with none of our ships working; it would almost be a relief to hear a ship's call sign cutting through the ether again. Of course the Dutch are making full use of our silence and one would think that they owned the air at times.

September 3rd, 1939 (*War with Germany is declared*)

S/S Indora: War was declared with Germany today. Now we are traveling under wartime precautions, windows painted black, etc. and we can have no lights shown. Here's to our success.

September 10th, 1939—S/S Indora

The Bombay docks are full of liners, tramps, coastal vessels, etc and there is a lot of activity mounting guns and camouflaging ships.

Sept. 19th, 1939—Karachi, India

Russia is now marching in on Poland as well—it looks rather bad. We expect to be chartered by the government for a trip somewhere soon. Quite a few troops are being shifted to Egypt from here.

Sept. 21st, 1939—Karachi, India—we are now loading Army lorries, guns, etc. for unknown destination.

Taken from *"The Signal Magazine"* (December 1939)—It saddened me to read about the loss of fellow radio officers.

"The news came to hand of the sinking of the *"Rawalpindi"*, with the loss of about three hundred lives. By this disaster, it is feared that we have lost three of our members, Messrs. S.W. Sharp, A. Emslie and D.S. Sutherland, First, Second and Third Radio Officers respectively. Messrs. Sharp and Emslie were men of over twenty years service, but Mr. Sutherland had not been as many weeks in the service. We deeply regret the anxiety which relatives and friends must be suffering, but until definite news is to hand, there is still hope. The *"Rawalpindi"* had only just relieved another ship on the northern patrol when she encountered the *"Deutschland."* She had no chance at all. With insufficient speed to escape, her guns out-weighted and out-ranged and no armour protection, her fate was sealed from the beginning. The action was all over in about 45 minutes and she sank a blazing wreck.

So far as the Radio Department was concerned, the ship was heard working for about fifteen minutes when a salvo from the *"Deutschland"* blew away the whole Bridge structure where the Radio Office was built. Up to the end the working was good and steady and our regret at this sad loss is tinged with pride that yet again our men carried on their duty."

Oct. 25th, 1939—Bombay

Yesterday the Chief Engineer, Captain and myself had to go to a conference at the sea Transport Headquarters for a meeting with the naval authorities. While there I met a chap named Miller who is the Radio Officer on the S/S Nuramahal an Asiatic line ship. He is a Scotchman from near John O'Groates—when he is at home. He is an ex University student at Edinburgh University who has tried fish farming and now is a Radio Officer. He has also done considerable Free Lance journalism and still carries on with that. We met again at Suez later on and had a good night at the Casino one night and the next day wandered about the town a bit.

We met again later on at Calcutta and went out to the Jain Temple together and took a few snapshots. It is a very ornate place and all the temple's fountains are covered with mosaic work. The Jains are a branch of the Hindu religion and do not believe in killing anything, even the tiniest of insects. A devout Jain will carry a small brush around with him and carefully brush around before he sits down so as not to kill any small insect. I have heard that if their beds get lousy they get a hairy man to sleep in it for a night and so carry them away without killing the lice. Of course I don't know how true that story is. There were many little statues all around the temple and it was most interesting. It was rather hot and tiring though and we soon grew tired of people begging for bakshish.

One day while in Calcutta, Kew (2nd Officer) and I went over the Hughly River to the Botanical Gardens. It is a nice place, well kept and well away from the clamorous crowd. Of course we had a look at the largest banyan tree in the world and thought it quite a tree. The banyan tree spreads by dropping its branches to the ground and these take root and start a new tree and so one tree can cover quite an area in this way. This particular tree covers several acres. We had a very pleasant tea at the tea rooms afterwards and then back to the ship.

A few days afterwards Kew got a shifted to another ship and I was extremely sorry to see him go as he is a grand chap and we have had some good times together. Our next port was Singapore and what a fine change it was after so much of India. The city is clean and surrounded by jungle covered hills. It is of course full of Chinese and to me the people and the place itself was very interesting. Ginger Street and I hired a taxi and made a tour around the place. One of the places we stopped at was the home of two rich Chinamen, a sort of show place I suppose. The house was very impressive and it was surrounded by a large wall that had many twisting passages cut through it with waterfalls, grottoes with little plaster elves in them and many interesting things. We thought it all very unique. His car was the *MOST* unique thing of all as it had the head of a large tiger where the radiator should be and a long stripped body and I should hate to meet it roaring along some dark road at night. We also visited the Botanical Gardens and found them very beautiful and full of very cheeky monkeys that wanted to be fed. The bamboos seemed to grow to an enormous size around there.

At night we visited the Raffles Hotel and began the evening well with several "stingas". Everybody seemed to be in evening dress despite the fact there there was a war on. There were a lot of Naval Officers about and we joined one party with a few friends of Gingers. Leaving there we went to the "Great World" the "New World" and several other places like that where I watched Ginger treading the "light fantastic" over the toes of pretty Chinese girls. The modern Chinese girl certainly knows how to

dress to best effect and they are very pretty. The harbor was very interesting with its many ships from all parts of the world. There were many Chinese junks and all the various assortments of native craft. It all looked
quite fascinating from up in the city where one could look down over it.

Our next port was Freemantle, Australia, and it looked pretty good after a
spell at sea. We were not there long but I took a bus over to Perth and had
a look around. Everyone there seems to live in quite comfortable circumstances and both places seemed to be made up of red roofed cottages. It
was good to see only white people again and all the girls looked positively
lovely after not having seen many white girls for so long. The Australian
accent is a bit hard to get used to; it is a bit like a mixture of Cockney and
American.

Next we called at **Adelaide,** a nice looking spot but we were not there long
enough to see much of it. Ginger and I took a bus up to the city and had a
look around during the afternoon. Ginger was complete in a green "pork-
pie" hat, a Malacca cane he had bought in Singapore and an odd colored
sport jacket. We did not intend going anyplace in particular and that must
have worried Ginger a bit as he kept stopping people and asking them the
way, then when they asked him where he wanted to go he would have to
admit that he did not know as he was a stranger.

Every now and then I would be breezing along quite merrily and I would
suddenly realize that Ginger was missing; looking around I would see him
asking the way from someone else. Eventually I suggested that he paint his
cane white the next time he came ashore. Anyway we had a good dinner
set off with a glass of good Australian port wine and then wandered out
and had a look at the park. Ginger's cane created rather a stir! I imagine
that only someone who looks as much like a prize-fighter as old Ginger
does could have got away with it without rude Australian remarks being
made. I think that even Ginger became a bit embarrassed with it at last as
he left it on board the next time he went ashore. The park turned out to be
rather nice with black swans swimming in the river and we could even sit

down on the grass and watch them—something you wouldn't dare to do in India.

Melbourne turned out to be a really nice place and I had a fine time there. The first night Brammall, Ginger Street and I went ashore and had dinner at Mario's where I tasted my first lobster and tried to eat my first oysters out of the shell. I didn't care much for the oysters, no doubt they are an acquired taste. One of the most interesting things to be seen in Melbourne is the old cable tram line that runs up Burke Street. A cable runs under the tram and between the tracks and when the tram is due to move the driver pulls a lever which makes something else grab hold of the cable and away you go with a jerk and a rattle. It runs for miles that way and I still do not understand how they manage it around the corners. I hear that it is soon to be replaced by a modern bus service or something.

I met some very charming people through Beasley, one of our Cadets. The Suttons made us feel very much at home and it was grand to talk to such friendly people of our own race again. They have a large and beautiful home near the outskirts of the city, or in the suburbs rather. There are two sons, one a dentist and the other going to school a daughter, Cynthia, who is a masseuse at the hospital here. Another young lady we met, Betty Taylor had just arrived back from the Los Angeles Exposition where station where she had been in charge of the Australian exhibits and we all accompanied her to the local broadcasting station where she made a recording of her experiences in the states. Mrs Sutton is a most motherly type of woman and wanted to know all about my people and what they thought of me wandering so far from home. We had a fine dinner and before I left Mrs. Sutton gave me the address of her sister at our next port with strict orders that I was to look her up and that they would be expecting me, which I thought was very nice of her. I also have a standing invitation to call at the Suttons whenever I come back.

I wandered around Melbourne quite a bit. One day I went out to a park that had Captain Cook's cottage. It was stone and very English in appearance. I also went to the Princess Street Bridge near Flinder's Station and took the ferry down to the Botanical Gardens, a beautiful spot where I loafed about to my hearts content and had a good tea.

I was very impressed with Sydney Harbor when we arrived there. It is a most attractive looking place with hills all around it and of course the first thing one sees is the famous Sydney Bridge. The first thing I did was to make a journey to it and look down on the city from one of its pillions in which is a camera obscura. All you have to do is look at it's face and you can see the various parts of the city while a lecture explains the points of interest as they roll around.

The next day was spent at the Wests as I had been asked out for the day. It was a splendid day. We went to Koala Park and I saw my first Koala Bears. They are about the cutest things I have ever seen and I bet they would make great pets. They can only live on a certain kind of gum tree leaf apparently but that is all they need as they never drink water. At one time they had been killed off for their fur until they were almost extinct: then the government stepped in and protected them. The park also contained a lot of kangaroos and wallabies. We had tea at Dr. Cowlishaws, the father of Dr. West's fiance and I met a lot more people and rather enjoyed it. I felt rather dazed after such a long spell of isolation on the Indian coast and never meeting anyone.

Another afternoon I went over to Karonga Park and wandered about. In the evening I went to a party at some cousins of Ginger Street. We had a rather stuffy time there but then I'm not great judge of parties. Anyway we met a couple of sisters that were quite good looking. We both made dates with them but I wasn't able to keep mine as we left before I expected. Ginger kept his and I think even proposed to the girl but fortunately for both of them she turned him down.

Next port of call was **Hobart, Tasmania**, a fine looking place with a large bay surrounded by hills and a red-roofed city lying at the foot of them along the bay. Before we called at Hobart itself we went up the river Durwin to a place called Risden where we took on some cargo. At Hobart I called at the Underhills, some friends of the Wests who had most kindly given me a letter of introduction to them. I enjoyed meeting them very much and the next day before the ship sailed Mr. Underhill took me for a drive around the city and part way up one of the mountains from where we had a fine view down over the city and bay. The countryside rather reminded me of Scotland.

Part 5
Back to India

o o o o o o o o o o o o o o o o o o o o o o o o o o o o o o o o o

Ah, with the Grape my fading
Life provide,
And wash my body whence
the Life has died,
And in a Winding sheet of
Vine-leaf wrapt,
So bury me by some sweet
Garden-side

(Rubaiyat of Omar Khayyam)

We called at Adelaide and Freemantle again and then we were off again across the Indian Ocean. I hated the thought of having to go back to India again but such is life. Our first stop was at Colombo and then on around to Trincomalee on the east coast of Ceylon. This is one of the most beautiful and unspoiled ports I have seen around the coast. It is surrounded by jungle and there is a nice little native village along the sea coast. There are many pretty bays running out from the main one, the water is a clear as crystal and the swimming is fine. It is nice to hear the birds calling in the jungle and the monkeys barking. It is very still at night and one can hear the frogs, crickets and other jungle noises. During part of the day the water is dead flat calm. Along the sea beach and part of the bay here are many palm trees. This place reminds me of Mergui and Moulmein. It is such a peaceful and beautiful spot and so unspoiled by civilization.

When we arrived at Madras an Indian Customs-walla came on board to seal my transmitter. I remarked that it was very warm. "Yes, he said, it is getting me down" so I began to wonder how I could be expected to stand it. The famous city of Madras is about the filthiest city in India and rather a shock to the senses of sight and smell after Australia.

How I hated arriving back in Calcutta again with its swarms of shouting, spitting coolies and its dust, smells, flies and heat. Captain Johnson left us there to go home on leave. When leaving he said that he would be glad to have me on any ship that was in his command. He is a fine ship-master and certainly knows his job.

Rangoon was our next port and it was rather nice to see it again with its pagodas and its cheerful, lazy Burmese. We were anchored in our usual place in the river. On the far side of flat paddy fields stretching into the distance and along the edge of the river are many teak mills. In the early morning it is very nice here as the sun rises like a great orange up through the morning mists and its rays glisten on the golden pagodas. Soon the sun becomes a coppery glare and very hot but in the evening it becomes very nice again and the sunsets over the river are magnificent and have to be seen to be appreciated; no paintings could do them justice.

One hot afternoon some of us visited the **Shwe Dagon Pagoda** and I took a lot more snaps. It was hot walking around that marble roadway in our bare feet. We were amused to see a Chinese Buddhist monk walking round and round the Shwe Dagon beating a drum and chanting. We were told that he did this a hundred times a day for over a week and was thereby earning great merit in heaven. That is one way of doing it anyway but I'll bet he has sore feet and a sore throat by the time he gets through.

One afternoon some of us visited a Burmese fair. The Burmese looked very gay indeed in their brightly colored clothes. I do not suppose that there is another race of people in the world that can wear such brilliant clothing as the Burmese without it looking in the least garish. In any other race such brilliant colors would seem outlandish if worn but not with the Burmese. The little Burmese women with the flowers in their hair, their brilliant dresses and the usual pretty parasol looked very attractive indeed. The only trouble is that they will rub some white paste made of the root of some tree over their faces which sometimes gives them rather a ghostly appearance. They made a gay and laughing crowd and it was good to mingle with them. I bought a Burmese dress dah and a couple of silk parasols and would have liked to have bought a lot more stuff only I cannot accumulate too many souvenirs or they will just have to be cast aside when I change ship. The dah was made in Upper Burma and the parasols came from Bassein. I also bought some nice mother-of-pearl work from Mergui.

After leaving the Burmese fair we decided to pay a visit to the Shwe Dagon by moonlight. Evening was setting in as we left the fair and a great full moon was just rising out of the east. We walked up Pagoda Road to the main stairway leading to the Shwe Dagon. At the top we found that we had the place nearly to ourselves except for a few belated worshipers. These were mostly chanting their evening prayers before the altars around the pagoda. The moonlight bathed the great Shwe Dagon and its hundreds of satellite pagodas with a golden glow, throwing dark shadows into the further corners of the courtyard. The fronds of the palm trees rattled slightly in the breeze and the same breeze stirred the tiny bells in the cupolas on the spire of each pagoda and they tinkled out their silvery refrain. A couple of temple policemen followed us as we wandered about, at a safe distance, and I have no doubt that they meant at all costs to prevent us running away with the forty ton bell.

Eventually we had to leave the pagoda of course and on the way back to the ship decided that it was high time to feed the inner man. We went to the Bombay Restaurant and gorged ourselves on chicken curry. It is amongst the places where a good native dish may be obtained and noted for its curries which are as hot as one could wish for. After that we took rickshaws down to the Sule Pagoda wharf and took a sampan back to the ship.

PERIOD COVERING APRIL 1ST TO NOVEMBER 30TH, 1940.

The first thing we knew we were back in Calcutta in the hottest most miserable time of the year in that horrible city. Dozens and dozens of Garden-Reach workmen were soon yelling, screaming and loudly clearing their throats in true oriental manner as they put steel plating all around my cabin to protect me from shell splinters and bullets. It looked like well worn ships plates though and I hadn't much faith in it. The pounding, riveting and welding went on day and night so I didn't get much sleep while there—between that and prickly heat. Indications were that I would get away from the coast at last and as I had had over two years foreign service in all and I was not the least sorry. Nearly all the officers were changed and people who were due leave replaced them. Captain Davis was our new Captain with mates Langdon, Hobson and Turk. We left Calcutta around the last of April and believe me it was great to get away from there.

Mauritius and the Dodo Bird

Our first stop was at Mauritius, a French speaking, British owned island off the coast of East Africa. I made haste to visit the local museum and trace the history of the famous, now extinct Dodo; a large and awkward bird that disappeared about three centuries ago. There were several reconstructed specimens there and an oil painting of one by a Dutchman who had actually seen them. They had swan shaped bodies, small wings and clean chicken shaped legs and feet, an odd looking bird that was entirely unable to defend itself in any way. After leaving the museum we went for a drive around a portion of the island in a taxi. We went out to Curepipe and passed many plantations of sugarcane and pineapple on the way. Much of the island seems to be made up of volcanic masses and we drove up to the upper lip of an extinct crater from where we had a fine view in all directions. After driving around a bit more we returned to our ship at Port Louis. The people at Mauritius are rather a mixture with French and

Indian blood predominating and probably a good percentage of Negro blood. It seems to be a fairly prosperous place though rather cut off from the world.

May 1940, Capetown

During May we arrived at Capetown after finding our way through a dense fog, and as we found out afterwards, an enemy minefield. We were very lucky indeed. When the fog eventually cleared away we saw Table Mountain looming up over everything and it looked a very imposing mountain with a flat top, thus the Table Mountain. The city itself surrounds the bay along the foot of the mountain. As soon as we got ashore we took a bus up to the foot of the mountain and then went to the top of the mountain by cable car; rather a breath-taking experience as you can look straight down for hundreds of feet at times and at others you pass right over smaller mountain peaks. I was very pleased when we reached the top safely. As the top of the mountain is 3,500 feet above sea level we had a pretty good view from there—the city down below and the sea stretching into the distance. Beasely and I went to church in the evening but were unfortunate in our choice as the parson must have had adenoids and bleated like a sheep. After church we followed the crowds to the city hall and it turned out that an orchestral concert was about to begin. It was a first class affair and I enjoyed it though I know less than nothing about music. Apparently those concerts are regular Sunday night affairs and they seem like a good idea to me. I rather liked Capetown with its many old fashioned houses, its mixture of British and Cape Dutch and the peculiar aroma of the Cape pipe tobacco as it is smoked.

June 1940 Port-Of Spain, Trinidad

During June we reached Port-of-Spain, Trinidad: ; a place with a very romantic sounding name. It makes you think of pirates and pieces-of-eight. On the way here we passed Tobago Island where some people claim Robinson Crusoe lived. One afternoon some of us hired a taxi to take us out to the famous Pitch Lake from which much of the road asphalt is obtained for roads all over the world. We had a fine drive out there through a very pretty countryside. There were flowering trees and shrubs all along the roadsides, hibiscus, flame of the forest, immortelle trees and many others. The driver told us that they planted immortelle trees amongst the cocoa trees to give them shade: we stopped at a cocoa orchard or whatever they call them and examined the pods of the cocoa bean, they are fairly large, contain several beans and the outside color varies but the ones I saw were red and green. We found Pitch Lake to be a low swampy looking spot partly overgrown with grass. There were several trucks out on it and negroes were digging out pitch and throwing it into the trucks. They told us that the holes they dug would be full up again in twenty four hours. They also said that at times they dug up well preserved skeletons of prehistoric animals. The Pitch Lake covers a hundred and ten acres and it looks as though there was no end to the asphalt in it. Some of the largest oil wells in the British Empire are near here and mean a lot to us now. The cocoa and sugarcane plantations seem to be the main thing in the way of agriculture around Trinidad. They also grow considerable grapefruit. The countryside is certainly beautiful around port of Spain and I enjoyed some very pleasant walks about it. I doubt if I could forget the smell of rum and molasses around those docks!

Bridge Town, Barbados

The next stop was Bridgetown, Barbados, but we were not there long. It is mostly a sugar producing island, sugar, rum and molasses. We tried several of the famous rum punches, they seemed as harmless as lemonade at the time but believe me they packed a punch all right. A harmless whiskey and soda will do me after that.

Kingston, Jamaica

We next arrived at Kingston Jamaica, a nice looking place with the Blue Mountains in the background. The waterfront smells quite fragrantly of rum, sugar and molasses. The Negroes do not look any too prosperous and some appear to be too well educated for the poorly paid jobs they are allowed to hold. All through the Indies I have had the impression that too many Englishmen and Scotchmen have made their fortunes out here and then taken it all away with them to their homeland where they set up as the local squires, leaving the land where they made their money that much poorer. I wouldn't be surprised if many of the Negroes there were not better off in the old slave days—at least someone looked after them. Turk and I met our ex-passenger from the Barbados at the Myrtle Bank Hotel and he introduced us to a bunch of other fellows working in banks and on plantations.

The Fall of France

During this time Belgium packed up fighting, Holland fell and France was negotiating with Germany for peace. Our army in France had to retreat and got out of France at Dunkirk but lost most of their equipment. Things looked bad all round and we were beginning to wonder if we have seen the last of the British Empire. Without the aid of the French fleet we knew we would have a tough time of it at sea. We left Kingston the day that France ceased fighting and I'm afraid we all took a rather poor view of it. The British Empire is left all alone now to fight Hitler's Germany. Churchill has taken over as Prime Minister of Great Britain and we all feel pretty good about that as he appears to be a fighter.

From my publication *"The Signal"* dated April, 1940, they wrote about Churchill: "Broadcasting on Saturday, January 20th, 1940, the First Lord of the Admiralty, Mr. Winston Churchill, said things have never gone so well in any naval war. It seems pretty certain that half the U-boats with which Germany began the war have been sunk, and that her new building has fallen far behind what we expected. For months past the Nazis had been uttering ferocious threats of what they are going to do to Britain and France when once they set about them, but so far the small neutral States were bearing the brunt of German malice and cruelty. The Dutch, the Belgians, the Danes, the Swedes and, above all, the Norwegians, were having their ships destroyed, not only by the blind and wanton mine, but by the coldly considered, deliberately aimed torpedo. Only in the British and French convoys could safety be found. There, the odds were five hundred to one against being sunk.

Addressing a crowded meeting in the Free Trade hall, Manchester, on Saturday, January 27th, 1940, Mr. Winston Churchill, First Lord of the Admiralty, said inter alia, *"Come then, let us to the task, to the battle and the toil—each to our part, each to our station. Fill the armies, rule the air, pour out the munitions, strangle the U-boats, sweep the mines, plough the land, build the ships, guard the streets, succour the wounded, uplift the down-cast and honor the brave. Let us go forward,* he concluded, *in all parts of the Empire in all parts of this island. There is not a week, nor a day, nor an hour to be lost."*

"I come before the House, on behalf of the Navy, to ask for a few men, some ships, and a little money, to enable them to carry on their work, which has become important to us all at the present time." He had, of course, to consider also merchant shipbuilding. *The need for increasing the number of men available is very great indeed. We are very concerned with the armament of our merchant ships. The question is simply how quickly these merchant ships can be armed. The first Lord informed the House that nearly two thousand merchant ships are armed by canon alone.*

I was pleased to see Havana, Cuba; particularly so as I had just finished reading *ANTHONY ADVERSE* with its vivid description of the old fort etc. and there it was right before my eyes—the old Fort, the old guns called the "Twelve Apostles" that used to guard the entrance to the harbor and the city of Havana. I expect that the city itself has changed a good deal since those days. We were not in Havana long but Turk and I had time to hire a taxi and have a look around the place. It is a beautiful city and looks quite prosperous; much more prosperous than the other West Indian islands that I have seen.

New Orleans, USA

Our next port was New Orleans. U. S.A. We could not get ashore for several days until special passports were provided for us. As our Captain managed to rub all the officials the wrong way I do not expect that sped things up at all. When we were eventually allowed ashore I went to the nearest bank to exchange some English Pounds. I found that no bank would tough them as the Yanks thought that Britain was going to fall and had no intentions of losing any money if they could help it! This was not a very cheering thought and I wondered what their reactions would be if I could have produced German Marks instead of British Pounds.

I was not much impressed with New Orleans or its people. The city itself is built on flat uninteresting country, the climate was sultry, hot and rainy—much like Rangoon but without its color and interest—and despite the many books I have read on southern hospitality I gained the impression that it might easily be governed by the amount of money that you cared to spend there. Of course a country or its people can hardly be judged by its seaports. They usually contain the worst of everything.

One afternoon I visited the museum with Beasely and found it quite interesting with many relics of the days when New Orleans belonged to France and of the Civil War of later days.

During our stay there we were pleased to hear that the British Navy had sunk a bunch of French Battleships that wouldn't surrender to us. That is a lot better than letting the Germans have them. France under Petain and Laval seems to be determined to help the Germans in every possible way. Our fleet will probably have more than it can handle as it is right now without the Germans getting more ships.

Torpedoes

On our way to the next port we managed to miss a German raider and were right glad of that. At Bermuda we waited for a few days until a small convoy gathered. We were anchored well out from shore and I only had one chance to get ashore. I went ashore with the Captain just before we sailed. It is quite a nice spot and has the advantage of having no automobiles to disturb things. However I am not exactly in the mood to appreciate things tropical after having been so long in India.

Leaving Bermuda we left in convoy and joined a much larger convoy later on off the east coast of America. Wireless reception was very good after the tropics. I heard a lot of distress calls from torpedoed ships and wondered if we would be next. We were carrying a cargo that could hardly stand that sort of thing. As we approached Britain's air, raider and submarine warnings became more frequent. We had quite a bit of bad weather and I found it pretty cool even though it was summer. A couple of hundred miles off Ireland we lost three ships through torpedo attack. They got two stragglers from our convoy during the night and the second ship ahead of us in the morning just as three destroyers were approaching us. The destroyers circled around like a terrier after a rat and they dropped a lot of depth charges. The torpedoed ship dropped astern and sunk as we were getting out of sight. The destroyers are supposed to look after picking up survivors so we did not stop. That same evening another ship reported seeing a torpedo track but fortunately it did not hit anything. When we reached the North Channel we were all feeling quite safe for once. *We had broken convoy to go through the channel and were just re-forming again when a destroyer rushed in just ahead of us and dropped three depth charges which nearly lifted us out of the water!*

It is probably a good thing that he got that sub as we were definitely the most likely target. About ten minutes later a plane spotted another sub not far away and dropped a depth charge on it and a destroyer dropped a few more depth charges as well. Anyway it all goes to show that danger is everywhere these days. There was a lot of wreckage floating about and I expect that a lot of ships had been lost. We arrived off Liverpool and anchored in the Mersey for the night and in time to hear the mournful wailing of the air raid sirens and see quite a display of searchlights in the sky as they tried to find the enemy planes.

Liverpool, England (August 1940) (Falling shrapnel and whistling bombs)

It was the first part of August when we arrived in Liverpool. I wandered about in the first black-out I had been in at night, heard my first whistling bombs and began to understand for the first time what war really meant. They had no heavy raids while I was there—just the odd plane every now and then that dropped the few odd bombs but you only have to get hit with a few odd bombs just once. Everyone expected Hitler to invade Britain at any moment and no one felt too good about that. Everyone seemed a bit stunned at the disaster that had befallen France but at the same time were fully determined to fight on. Things looked very dark and dreary indeed but everyone hoped that something might happen to see us through it. Every night we had several air raids. First we would hear the mournful howl of the sirens as they wailed out their warning to take shelter. Then we would hear the drone of the plane, perhaps see the searchlights running across the clouds in search of it and likely hear the deafening noise of our guns when they found the plane. The danger from falling shrapnel from our own shells was almost as great as from enemy bombs at times. During one raid I looked overboard and remarked about the numerous fish jumping, then suddenly we realized it was shrapnel falling so we kept our heads under cover after that.

I would have liked to have gone home on leave but things were so bad at that time and every man needed that I could hardly ask to go home. As our ship had been specially fitted up for a certain run it was likely that she would be kept on the North Atlantic run so I asked to stay on her in the hopes that if she did go to Halifax or Montreal I might get a few days leave. I would surely like to see the folks at home again.

I went to the theater a couple of times in Liverpool and generally enjoyed myself as much as possible under the circumstances. I met quite a few chaps just back from Dunkirk and believe me, they have had a pretty bad time of it. *This time was indeed Britain's grimmest hour but everyone had great faith in Churchill, he was the man of the hour.*

The weather was damp and chilly in Liverpool. I caught a cold and felt generally miserable and wished for the warmth of the tropics again. Another night we were nearly hit by a whistling bomb. It came down over our masts and dropped on the sheds between us and the ship on the other side. Another bomb dropped on the overhead railway outside the docks and another fell on a lock gate. All of them were too close for comfort. Another night Woods, Dexter (new 2nd and 3rd mates) and myself were just returning from a night up town and had reached the dock gates when the sirens went and we could hear the drone of an approaching plane. We all, including the gate policeman, made for the nearest shelter. The searchlights lit up the sky like day, the guns made a terrific row and no one could resist the temptation to watch it from the entrance of the shelter. We saw the plane caught in the searchlights and the tracer bullets and flaming onions climbing up after it and even the policeman was jumping up and down and shouting with glee as they passed close to the plane. The next morning we read in the papers that they had knocked one engine out of the plane but couldn't find the plane itself. Later we heard that the plane had crashed in Ireland.

Swansea *(night in an air-raid shelter)*

Our next port was Swansea, a rather pretty place set amongst the hills. There were both day and night air raids there and the sirens seemed to be going all the time. There I learned to my disappointment that we were going back out east again but in war time you have to take whatever comes your way and like it. Today completes one full year of war. *If our shipping losses continue at this rate Britain will starve. The Merchant vessels bring food, armament and other supplies to Britain and if the navy cannot protect us Britain may well be doomed.*

September the 2nd Exploding bombs in Swansea.

We had gone through one of the heaviest blitzes to date and the center of the city was heavily hit. The blitz lasted for six and a half hours and the planes came over in waves about every ten minutes. The air seemed full of screaming bombs and I can tell you that I never expected to live until morning. The city seemed a blaze of fire from the hundreds of incendiary bombs and I thought that the city would be a mass of burning ruins by morning. However when morning eventually did arrive it was difficult to see the damage. A pal of smoke overhung the city for several days after that. The center of the city was the hardest hit and the streets were covered with broken glass from the shop windows. Many buildings were smashed beyond repair. The emergency crews did a wonderful job. It was rather a weird experience to see great buildings flung up into the air by the force of the exploding bombs. Quite a a number of bombs hit around the docks but mostly on open land and a few incendiaries fell into the water. It was the middle of the city that really got hit. The night seemed to drag through very slowly and it seemed as though morning would never come. The all-clear went about half past four in the morning. During the night there had been remarkably little gun-fire or searchlights in action and everyone was pretty puzzled by it. We just stay on the ship during air raids; all the shelters are quite far away and mighty uncomfortable places. It looks like a bleak future for these cities if they keep having raids like that. Still, the people seem to take it well and will probably see it through to the bitter end in the good old British way.

The night after the raid we went up town when the sirens began. The streets were soon cleared and we followed a bunch of people into a public shelter. They were a cheerful lot and we were entertained by a bunch of Jack-tars for some time who put on a dancing act. We noticed that quite a few people appeared to be living in the shelter and we learned later that they had lost their homes in the last raid. Many people were in that shelter and it had poor ventilation so after a few hours it had that oppressing smell of packed humanity. Many of the men had just been returning to their home from work and I wondered how they could carry on during the days if they got much of that. Not only was the ventilation bad but people had to sit on the floor, also the sanitary arrangements were most inadequate for such a large and mixed crowd. Along towards midnight people started sleeping on the floors and I felt sorry indeed for the women and little children. In the middle of the night I got pretty fed up with it there and offered to see a nurse back to her hospital as she had to go on duty. By the time I did that and made the long walk back to the docks. It was just on daybreak and the all-clear was going. There seemed to be no let-up from the wailing of those sirens either day or night. I take my hat off to plain, ordinary John Citizen if he can carry on through that stressful life.

Leaving Swansea and then Milford Haven the *S.S. Indora* was escorted for a period out into the Bay of Biscay and then turned back after signaling "good luck" as we headed out into the Atlantic and southward around South Africa. It was good to get back to tropical seas. We passed close enough to Cape Town to see Table Mountain. We eventually arrived at Durban and it was very pleasant to get a couple of nights sleep. We had been keeping four hour watches at first but had to change to six on and six off after a while as we were just about wandering around in a daze from lack of sleep after the first few days. Even the six hours on and off were pretty tiring. We found Durban to be a very pretty place and it looked particularly good from the sea. It was Sunday so we had a look around the place during the day. At night Beasley and I went to a concert at the City Hall. The orchestra was made up of local talent and members of the Royal Marine band from a visiting warship. It was a good concert and reminded me of Cape Town. The South Africans seem to be very fond of music. We all wish that we could stay around this part of the world for a bit longer but on we must go.

Penang, Malaya and Musings about Japan Possibly Entering the War

After an uneventful voyage across the Indian Ocean and the Bay of Bengal we arrived at **Penang, Malaya** and it seemed that we were well and truly back East again. It begins to look as though Japan was determined to enter the war on Germany's side so the question is where will she start and what will the East be like then. It does not look at all reassuring out this way. Europeans take life too easy and most of them are quite convinced that war can never touch them. Some fine day they may easily wake up to find that the world has been moving on while they slept.

Penang is without doubt one of the most beautiful places I have seen in the East and it must be a grand place to live. Despite my criticism of the people out here the Europeans in this place are surely friendly and very different indeed to those that we do meet in India. We have been made temporary members of their swimming club and soon got to know people. In India you could call at ports all your life and probably never get to know anyone so we appreciate finding this different atmosphere in the East.

November 4th, 1940—Penang, Malaya

We are anchored well out in the Roads here and have to get ashore by sampan which is a sure sign that we are well and truly back East. We are anchored in a well protected bay and the water is very calm and clear. The shore is about three quarters of a mile away and we envy the steamers that are fortunate enough to be laying alongside the Swettenham Pier which is right handy to the city. Have just found out that the actual name of this place is not Penang though it is marked as such on the map. Penang is actually the whole island on which this place is situated and the city itself is called George Town. It stretches back from the waterfront at the foot of a range of hills along which the white clouds hang during the early morning.

One of the sights worth seeing here is the many junks with their sepia-colored and shell-shaped sails as they sail in and out of the bay. With the city and the hills in the background as seen from the bay here they make a most picturesque sight. Most of the sampan wallas are Chinese though a few of them are Indians and the sampans are rather larger than at Rangoon.

Nov.5th, 1940: George Town, Penang

This morning I went ashore with my Junior and one of the Naval Ratings. It takes around twenty five minutes to get ashore by sampan and when we neared the jetties we were we were greeted by the overpowering smell of very bad fish, junks that needed cleaning out, and various other typical smells of the East. Taxis and jinrikishas seemed to be the most popular methods of getting about and the most popular of the two are the jinrikishas. These will hold two people with ease and are lavishly decorated with flowers, dragons and even parrots which are painted on the backs and sides of the jinrikishas. The place is definitely a Chinese city and the Malayans and the ever-present Indians are only to be seen in small numbers in comparison. During the past half century the Chinese have flooded into the Malay States and have rather pushed the easy-going Malayans into the background as far as Industry and trade is concerned. Personally I think they are much to be preferred to the Indians and certainly George Town is a cleaner and nicer city then any Indian city ever can hope to be.

We wandered about doing a bit of shopping though it was too hot to feel very energetic. Murphy, the Naval Rating, secured a driving permit so that we may hire a car to drive about in and then we dropped into the Eastern and Oriental Hotel for a drink and to cool off a bit. It is certainly hot and sultry in this part of the world. During the morning the sun beats down full force and during the afternoon the rain usually beats down full force but it does not get any cooler. The nights are sultry and hot as well but during the early morning hours it cools off a bit. The others stayed up town and went to the pictures but it was so hot that I decided to seek the comparative coolness of my cabin and so came back to the ship between afternoon showers.

Nov.6th, 1940: George Town, Penang

Today the three Naval Ratings, the 2nd Radio Officer and myself hired a car and with Murphy driving we set out to see what we could see. There is a road that runs completely around the island and we set out on that via the Northern Road. Soon we were climbing up amongst the hills and the many rubber plantations along the wayside. The scenery was magnificent and we had many fine views down over the valleys and the paddy fields along the coast. There were many hairpin bends in the road and in places it ran along steep high hills with several hundreds of feet sheer drop if the car ran off the road. That did not deter Murphy in the least however and he seemed to consider them a challenge to his skill as a driver. I'm sure he averaged at least forty five miles an hour around each bend. At length we passed down to more level traveling where the rubber trees were larger than along the hills. At one place where the rubber trees were tapped we stopped to see just how it was done. A groove had been cut half way round the tree and this slanted downwards at one end. This groove had been cut in the bark of course and not into the tree itself. At the lower end of the groove a rounded tin spike had been driven in just under the cut: an earthenware pot was set under the spike to catch the milk-like rubber as it flowed down the cut in the bark, the pot was set on another piece of tin that had been driven into the tree below the spike. The grooves had been cut in the bark of the trees so that the outside bark was the highest and the rubber sap flowed around the tree to the spike without overflowing down the side of the tree. Each of the earthenware pots would hold almost a pint of rubber sap I should imagine.

The houses in Malaya are built upon stilts the same as in Burma; they are rather more ornate however with very fancy wood carving upon some of them. We gradually left the rubber forests and came out into flat paddy land where the green and half grown paddy stretched for miles. Gradually we came into more settled country and so back into George Town once more after a most interesting forty five mile drive. We also visited the waterfall just outside of the town. This place is called the Waterfall Gardens and it is a really pretty spot. We could see the waterfall tumbling down the rocks from a distance but the roadway that led up along it was "closed until further notice." The place seemed to swarm with monkeys and they all came down out of the trees to see us.

Then we went down to the Church Street Ghaut Jetty and drove on board the ferry steamer and in due time were landed at Bagan Luar (Mitchell Pier), this pier being on the mainland. We had no idea as to where we wanted to go when we crossed over but on landing we saw a sign reading

"Taiping 8 miles" so we decided to go there. The road was good and stretched through miles of low laying land where forests of rubber trees covered the land. Water lay in the ditches along the roadway and the rubber forests had deep ditches dug between the trees. We saw natives fishing in the ditches and using nets as well and I thought how handy it must be to step-out of a palm thatched hut and catch a meal so easily right at the front doorstep, or else to just knock a few coco-nuts down from the nearest palm tree. No wonder the Malayans are inclined to take life easy. The land through the rubber forests was so low and swampy that I can now quite understand why a rubber planter's story usually includes many bouts of malaria during his stay in Malaya.

The isolated huts and the little villages along through the rubber forests seemed to be occupied by Malays but the larger villages and towns that we passed through seemed to be inhabited chiefly by Chinese. We passed through Bagan Serai about thirty-four miles from Penang, then through Sei Gedong; about thirty nine miles out and through Simpan Ampat which was about forty one miles along the way as well as numerous other towns and villages. We passed through a series of hills during the later part of our journey and then back into more level country where it was very swampy. They were dredging for tin in places. This was something new to me as I always thought that tin had to be dug out of hillsides and suchlike. We arrived at Taiping just at sunset and had just time to drive around before it got dark. It is pretty well all Chinese as far as the shops in it are concerned; the Chinese seem to be everywhere one goes here in Malaya. We tried to find someplace to eat but they do not seem to advertise the hotels in such places and I suppose there are so few Europeans that it is quite unnecessary. So we decided to head back for Penang and eat when we arrived there. Murphy drove like mad on the way back despite my feeble protests. All went well until we tried sailing around a corner in the glare of an approaching car and we ended by pushing a concrete corner post down into a steep ditch. We straightened the bumper of the car out as best we could and proceeded on our way, very thankful that we had not followed the corner-post down into the water-filled ditch. It had been raining all afternoon and it rained all the way back to Penang but even that did not dampen our pleasure in the trip.

Arriving back in Penang we had a late dinner at the Swiss Café and then left the car at the docks and walked back to the jetties where we found a sampan walla and so arrived back at the ship after a most satisfying day in the way of seeing things.

November 10th/1940—Penang, Malaya

Today the 2nd, 3rd Mates, 3rd Engineer, 2nd Radio Officer and myself decided to spend the Sunday ashore and so proceeded to do so. First of all we hired a taxi for the day and then went out to the swimming club for a swim. It was a nice place and supposed to be quite exclusive or something; we had all been given honorary membership for the duration of our stay there. In addition to a swim I know that I have acquired a good sunburn. The people there were much more friendly than they usually are out east and we appreciated that.

Leaving the Swimming Club we then had tiffin at the Swiss Café after which we proceeded out to the hills to the foot of the Hill Railway as we wanted to go to the top of the hills and apparently that is the only way up there. The hills reach to about 2400 feet above sea level at the top and as we went up we had a marvelous view down over the countryside. Half way up we changed to another car at the center station and that took us to the top. Each track has two cars and as one goes up the other car (which is on the other end of the cable) comes down and they pass at a double track half way up. They go up at a very steep incline and one seems to fairly hang over the valley below. At the top we wandered along a roadway and enjoyed the fine scenery below as well as the comparative coolness to the hot sultry climate at the bottom. I suppose it must have been all of ten degrees cooler up there. There were some fine houses at the top which is where the rich Europeans and Chinese live. The houses all had fine surroundings as well and the houses seemed to blend into the scenery they were so tastefully built. As we came down the hill railway it started to rain as that seems the usual thing for it to do in the afternoon in Penang. We returned to the Eastern and Oriental Hotel until the pictures started and then went and saw a very poor picture and so ended our Sunday ashore.

Nov. 14th/1940—Penang, Malaya

We are leaving here tomorrow and must confess that I will be rather sorry to leave such a beautiful and peaceful looking spot. It has been nice being back in a world where there are no air raids, no bombs falling and no black-outs. In fact they don't seem to know that there is such a thing as a war on out here. Also the mere fact that we are back out East again seems rather pleasant though I am sure that I could never manage to explain why that is so.

November 21st/1940: Calcutta, India

Here we are back in Calcutta once more—our old home port. We are tied up at Esplanade moorings just opposite the Eden Gardens and of course in the Uglis River. It is the cool season here now and is certainly the nicest time of the year. It seemed quite familiar to be pushing my way through the swirling chattering crowds once more; to see and hear the hundreds of beggars showing their deformed limbs and whining for bakshish and to see the ever present holy cattle wandering sedately about the crowed streets. The streets are all as red as ever from the betel nut juice that the Indians delight in spitting over everything and all in all its just the same old Calcutta, even to the carrion crows that perch everywhere with mournful croaks and the vultures that circle high in the sky overhead.

November 1940: Calcutta

During November 1940, we arrived back in Calcutta once again. Things looked quite familiar but I cannot say that I was overjoyed at arriving back in India again. We moored at Esplanade moorings nearly opposite Eden Gardens and it was quite a nice spot and very handy to up-town. We were lucky to arrive back during the cool season. The swarming crowds of natives, the noise and the clamor and the dust and dirt all seemed a bit too familiar even after several months absence though I suppose there is something about it all that has its attractions. There is a certain humid, sultry atmosphere about Calcutta that is even reflected in the lazy calls of the thousands of carrion crows. Betel nut chewing crowds of natives loaf along the streets spitting copious streams of bright red betel nut juice all over the pavements, crowds make way for the sacred cows as they wander through the streets and beggars still swarm as thickly as the carrion crows. Beasley and I had a good-bye party after nearly a year together on the same ship. We did everything from the Marine Club to the Continental and had dinner at Firpos. My Jr. Radio Officer was transferred to another ship. I was rather glad to see him go and so get back to eight hour watches again.

Rangoon again:

It was good to get back to Rangoon again as I really like Burma. The Shwe Dagon looked as beautiful as ever and the brown sailed barges, the sampans, the tugs pulling rafts of teak down the river and the fascinating sunsets over the Irrawaddy still had the same old fascination. They started replacing Indian cargo coolies with Burmese ones as the Burma Government has made that a new regulation and a certain number of them have to be employed. As the Burman's idea of work is five minutes work and fifty-five minutes sleep they are not very popular with the Mates. The 3rd claims to have found them fast asleep in the bilges with the water up to their waist. *"Will they work, Will they Hell"*, said the 3rd in disgust.

Moulmein

The anchor chain rattled out through the hawse-pipe as we came to anchor off the beautiful, palm-clad town of Moulmein. Back of the town stretched a high verdure-covered hill that ran parallel to the river. Along the top of the hill, standing silhouetted against the sky, stood several white pagodas. At the far end of the hill we could see a golden pagoda surrounded by many temples. The Chief Engineer who was standing by my side, started to hum the words of Kipling's immortal *"Mandalay"* and I wondered just which pagoda could be the *"Old Moulmein Pagoda, lookin' lazy at the sea"*.

Soon the work of loading our cargo of teakwood and rice began, accompanied by the incessant rattling of our winches and the chanting of our cargo coolies. The Second Officer and I decided to escape from the noise of cargo work for the afternoon by going ashore so we hailed one of the queer shaped Burmese sampans passing by and shortly we were stepping ashore at one of the river jetties. It was hot and sultry ashore so we looked about for some method of conveyance. There were several Madrassi gharry-wallas about with their Victorian-looking carriages and little ponies so we jumped into a garry and were soon whirling along through the crowded streets to the bazaar.

We found the bazaar to consist of many buildings that sprawled along the river front in a haphazard sort of way. In one corner of the bazaar we found piles of bark hats; they had wide slanting brims and their pointed tops were tipped with tin. A cheerful little Burman, who spoke excellent English, told us that the bark hats were mostly worn by the river boatmen and the paddy field workers during the monsoon season. We strolled on and came to the cheroot portion of the bazaar where cheroots of all lengths and sizes were for sale. Some of them were made up with the black strong-smelling tobacco that places the Burmese cheroot in a class by itself the world over while the cheroots that were more favored for local consumption were made of chopped up tobacco rolled in white corn husks. Many of the cheroots were as long as eight inches and it is rather startling to see a dainty little Burmese maiden calmly puffing away at such an over-sized cigar, for in Burma the women are just as heavy smokers as the men. We walked on into another section of the market and discovered much in the way of Burmese handicrafts. There were finely carved alabaster images of Buddha, beautiful Burmese parasols, hand carved ivory work, and rows of wicked looking Burmese dahs that were all bright and shiny and ready for use.

On leaving the bazaar we decided to go to the teak mill, or rather to one of the numerous teak mills that dot the river bank and watch the elephants at work handling the huge logs. To this end we hailed a passing bus but before proceeding further perhaps I had better explain about the Moulmein buses for surely they are unique in a world of buses. They consist of Moulmein made bus bodies which are tied nailed and bolted upon rather dubious second hand automobile frames and contain many various sorts of engines. They are built to hold about ten passengers but they are invariably so packed with humanity that the occupants appear to be almost bulging out of the windows. Now the bus also serves as a taxi in Moulmein so that when one wants a taxi it is quite in order to hail a passing and well filled bus that right willingly pulls up and after a bit of bargaining with the driver why the price is set for an hour or two hours or half a day as the case may be. Then the driver informs the passengers that their bus ride is off and gives them back their fares. With the calm philosophy of their race they climb out, light up their cheroots, and squat down by the side of the road to wait for the next bus. Such was the procedure in our case and we climbed into our bus-come-taxi and started on our way amidst a grinding of gears and much honking on the horn. The Burmese bus driver is apparently as reckless in his driving as his bus is makeshift. We clung to our seats and tried to look as though we were used to it while the bus tore through the crowded streets; missing gharrys by inches, making rickshaw-wallas jump for their lives and swerving around corners amidst a screeching of brakes and more dismal bellows from the ancient hand operated horn. The driver seemed bent upon our immediate and final destruction so that it was with a feeling of pleasant surprise that we found ourselves coming to a jerky and sudden stop before the gate of the teak mill.

Within the mill yards the air was filled with the fragrance of freshly sawn teak. Passing through one of the sheds we came to the water's edge where the huge teak logs were being drawn from out of the river with a revolving chain. After the logs were released from the chain at the top they were rolled and pushed to the various saws by one of the largest elephants I had ever seen. The whine of the many large circular saws filled the air as they ate their way through the great teak logs. We followed the course of the logs through the mill, watching them as they passed from saw to saw until at last they finished their journey in the shape of scantling, planks, and board; ready to be shipped to many parts of the world where teak is very highly valued. We watched several elephants at work as they carefully stacked the sawn lumber into its various places. They used their steel protected tusks to raise the teak off the ground and no length of timber seemed too heavy for them to lift as though it were only a match stick. They did their work with scarcely a guiding touch from the Indian mahouts who sat on their backs. No doubt, I reflected, these same elephants had handled much of the teak that had gone to build the sailing ships of other days; ships that had sailed the world in search of trade and adventure. As we were leaving the mill yard one of the elephants stopped to salaam us; looking up we saw that its mahout was also busy making profound salaams from his lofty perch so we threw him the always expected bakshish.

After another short but exciting drive with our reckless bus driver we parted with him at the foot of the hill that overlooks Moulmein and proceeded up the steep path on foot. At length we reached the top from where the stately white pagodas keep their seemingly eternal vigil on the countryside below. As we strolled along the summit of the hill the sounds from far below drifted faintly up to us as though from another world. From the monastery near the golden pagoda came the mellow tones of a Burmese gong. Several Buddhist monks, wearing saffron colored robes and carrying their wooden begging bowls, passed us as they returned to their monastery. The welcome breeze that broke the sultry heat of the afternoon also moved the little bells hanging from the cupola of a nearby pagoda. The fascination of their musical tinkling notes kept us standing there until the breeze dropped again. From where we stood we could look down over miles of absolutely flat paddy land that was broken again in the distance by the peculiar high hills that rise so precipitously from the other wise flat country side around Moulmein. Looking over the river we could see the old town of Martaban with its large white pagoda perched on a high cliff by the water's edge. It was growing late as we started to go down the steep pathway again and the sun was beginning to sink like a glowing ball of fire behind the western horizon. It stained the sky with various shades of orange and yellow and purple that were reflected again in the water of the river below. Behind us the monastery gong once more sent its mellow notes vibrating through the stillness of the evening air; as the sound gradually faded away the silence of the evening seemed to hang heavily over the pagoda hill, or perhaps it was the brooding spirit of the ages past standing guard over the pagodas upon the hill that we felt. That spirit must jealously guard the peace and beauty of the hillside and the colorful land of Burma stretching out below.

My last visit to Moulmein was during December, 1940. Since then we have seen many changes in the east and perhaps we will never see these things again as they were before the war. A few weeks go we were in Rangoon when we heard that Moulmein had fallen to the Japanese. Later we met refugees from there who told us that there was scarcely a building in Moulmein that had been left undamaged by bombs. We heard that one of the teak mill elephants had run amuck during a heavy air raid. There were tales of the gallant and fierce fight put up by our troops against overwhelming odds. The thunder of guns and the crash of bombs had truly broken the peace of Burma's countryside. Now it is war to the finish.

Those pagodas on the hill looked pretty good again and I felt glad to be back. I doubt if anything short of a war will ever change the peacefulness of this spot or the beauty of it. I hope that nothing ever changes it because it is one of the most unspoiled and beautiful spots I know of.
Silvrdale and the Trevenum here give you the impression that time has stood still for several hundred years, but that is a rather nice thing I think.

One morning I went ashore armed with my camera, the Captain's exposure meter and the firm resolve to get some more good snaps of elephants working in the teak mills. First of all I climbed up the hill over-looking the town that has the pagodas on it. I visited the Pagoda that Kipling is said to have meant when he wrote "Mandalay". I took off my shoes and climbed the stairway guarded by two stone lions. The platform surrounding the pagoda was quite large and at intervals medium sized bells were hung near the edge. These could be beaten with stag horns that were there for that purpose. The bells are mentioned in Kipling's book *"From Sea to Sea"*. I noticed some rather unique drawings in the temples at one side of the platform. One drawing of some very starved looking people with their bones showing was no doubt meant to represent the Burman's idea of Hell. As most Burmese are fairly plump it would no doubt have to be pretty hard times to starve. Next I stopped a bicycle and side-car and had him take me to the bazaar. I wandered around through the dim rickety old buildings; through the portions where the stone and alabaster Buddha idols were sold, past the parasol and the cheroot sections and ended up by buying a bamboo pipe. After that I left the bazaar and had a garrywalla drive me out to one of the teak mills where I took a lot more snaps of the elephants at work. They are certainly skilled workers and it was absolutely fascinating to watch the way they piled the teak and stacked it wherever necessary. At length I reluctantly dragged myself away from there and so back to the ship.

It was full moon during our stay at Moulmein and it was a beautiful sight to see it rise up behind the pagoda hill with the pagodas silhouetted against the sky. There is something quite fascinating about Burma in its own way; whether it is just the atmosphere, the climate or the people I do not know but I suppose they all combine.

Mid December, 1940 ... Bassein

About the middle of December 1940 we arrived at Bassein. Only a few Europeans live there so the place is quite unspoiled. The Burmese surely know how to wear their brilliant colored clothes, no other people could even attempt to wear such bright colors without looking silly but not the Burmese—it suits them. It is interesting to watch the various river craft on the river here, there are so many kinds and types; everything from small sampans to fair sized junks. It is also interesting to watch the steady flow of traffic along the river front rickshaws seem to be the favorite method of conveyance here. There are many clumps of bamboos along the river and they look quite attractive. At this time of the year the paddy (rice) was just being cut and as we came up river we could see the oxen trampling round and round on the grain in many places to thresh it in what I suppose is the oldest method in the world. Along the river about Bassein is a very fertile portion of the country and a lot of rice is grown there. Rice mills are situated along the river bank in many places. This is our main cargo of course and a steady stream of bags of rice flows on board, each bag carried by a coolie, an endless human chain. Most of the work like that is done by the Indian coolies of course as the Burman has a most healthy aversion to work of any kind.

We had Christmas day at sea as per usual but we had a good dinner anyway. I'm afraid Christmas is inclined to fall a bit flat unless one is home for it. We were in Cochin for New Years day but we did not get ashore. The main things of interest here are the huge dip nets that the natives use for catching fish in along the entrance to the harbor: also the fact that there are a tribe of Jews there that no one can trace the origin of—wonder if they are the lost tribe?

Jan.31, 1941 Rangoon

The last of January 1941 found us back at Rangoon again. We went out of the city to a large stone Buddha about sixty feet or more high and I took a couple of snaps of that. The sunrises and sunsets on the Rangoon river here are surely grand. No painting could quite do justice to them. I always find the river traffic quite fascinating to watch as well.

We had an accident as we were coming alongside the jetty at Bhavnagar. A fairlead gave way forward and a steel hauser leading to the jetty snapped tight and killed the Serang and one of his men. It happened about two o'clock in the morning and I heard the chanting and wondered what it was at first. It was the other kalassis chanting over the dead. We had a nice drive out around the town of Bhavnagar with Fernandes the stevedoring contractor one afternoon. We had tea afterwards at his house and met his wife and little daughter. He is a most intelligent person and always willing to discuss Indian politics so is quite interesting. He is a Goaness.

In March we were at Akyab, Burma loading more rice. It was a long way to shore from where we were anchored but the fourth Engineer and I went one afternoon. Akyab is a very lazy sort of a place. Many of the bungalows had old fashioned punkas in them that swung to and fro whenever the punkas walla wakes up to pull the cord.

April 1941 (Rangoon) My Unfortunate Accident

And so back to Rangoon again where I met with an unfortunate accident. I managed to bump my pet forehead against a steel bullet-proof plate that angled out into the center of the cabin to protect the wireless room. The plate did not bend by my forehead did so I ended up at the hospital. A Major Raymond operated on me the next day and managed to straighten things up fairly well for which I was very grateful. He did it using a local anesthetic and it was rather interesting as I lay there all covered over with sterilized sheets. I remember feeling quite indignant when a doctor from another wing came in and asked if I was a man or a woman …

My head was a mess of bandages for some days. They had cut the roof out of my eye to do the operation and then replaced it. The cut was made across my left eyebrow and took a lot of stitches to close up. After it was over with I had to lie with my head between a couple of sandbags for a couple of days to keep me laying on my back. As the temperature was about a hundred and two in the shade and I had a bit of a temperature at first it wasn't very comfortable and my back was a mass of prickly heat. The Burmese and Anglo-Burmese and Anglo-Indian nurses were all very good to me indeed. After the first couple of days when I could move my head around a bit I really enjoyed it and thought it was a fine holiday.

While I was in hospital the Burmese celebrated their Water Festival which consists of throwing water over everything and everybody. This is supposed to bring them luck. Never heard such a racket as went on outside that hospital for three days and nights. The people never seemed to cease shouting or the bands to cease playing. The Burmese certainly do enjoy themselves when they get going. Transportation in the city practically ceased during this time as bus and taxi owners would not risk getting the insides of their vehicles ruined with water.

I was in hospital for about twelve days and my head healed up very nicely. In the meantime the ships agents had been frantically phoning up every day to see when I could join a ship as they were a man short. Anyway the Doc said that I would be OK to go back to work as long as I took life easy for a while so I joined the *Warina.*

I had a rather weird experience while in hospital. One day after I had been there about a week the Doctor came along and removed the stitches. As he was leaving he stood by the door and remarked that he would be seeing me. A table laden with surgical instruments stood there with a nurse beside it. Suddenly I realized that I had seen this exact scene before, the Doctor saying those exact words, the table with the surgical instruments and the nurse standing by it. Then I remembered dreaming this very scene about a week before the accident happened. Of course I paid little attention to it and had practically forgotten all about it until it was suddenly recalled by the scene repeating itself in the hospital. Ordinarily I do not dream much. Anyway I hope I don't have any more dreams like that! Obviously at some level in my dream state I had the ability to see into the future and I'm not sure if I like being able to have that talent!

Our first stop was Karachi in my new ship and some of us went ashore to the pictures and had Dinner at the Bristol Hotel. I found a very good crowd on the ship. Next we arrived at Bahrein, a new spot for me, however we anchored off-shore as usual so did not see much. After leaving Bahrein we went to Rastanura, about forty miles on up the coast where we again anchored off-shore. Some of the Arab shippers looked a pretty tough crowd with cartridge belts slung around their shoulder and plenty of cartridges which are very valuable in places like that. It was very hot there with a lot of flies.

Back to Bombay again in May and the weather very hot and sultry and everyone had prickly heat. Things were not so good in Bombay at that time as there were quite a few riots and people getting killed. Next we arrived at Cochin after getting a bit of a dusting in the first of the monsoon on the way down. This ship is most uncomfortable in rough weather as she is very wet and has a very lively motion so that there is little comfort on her.

June, 1941—Back in Burma

We arrived back at Bassein during June, 1941. It was nice to be back in Burma again. The first night we were anchored in the river with no work so it was nice and peaceful with just the frogs croaking along the river bank and the creaking of the oars of the occasional sampan. During the evenings Lucas and I used to go for walks and very nice they were. There are so many things to see in Burma; sights and sounds and smells and always something different. Usually on our walks we would be followed at a distance by a couple of hopeful rickshaw-wallas. By walking we were of course deliberately taking the bread right out of their mouths, or so they said. Sometimes we would circle out into the country amongst the paddy fields. One thing I have often noticed has been the natives fishing amongst the flooded paddy fields. Sometimes they fish with hook and line and sometimes they pull a net along the ditches. They must catch something otherwise they would not do it but I have not yet managed to see what it is they catch—probably a type of catfish. The sunsets are very pretty here just now with the heavy monsoon clouds hanging in the west.

July, 1941 (Cochin)

We arrived at Cochin about the first of July, 1941. We had had a stormy passage so it was nice to get into port. We anchored off the old walk. The old British town of Cochin was owned by the Dutch and the Portuguese in turn before the British and it shows marks of the occupation of both. The many canals running through the place gives it a very Dutch atmosphere.

Lucas and I went for a walk one evening and I will set down my impressions of just an ordinary stroll through Cochin:

Just an ordinary stroll through Cochin:

We went ashore in a hired boat and a multitude of rickishaw wallas and whining beggars besieged us as we stepped onto the wharf. We walked away from the jetty followed by some very persistent rickishaw wallas who pointed out that it was not good for the Sahibs to walk. Some very small and very curious boys followed us.

We came to a small canal with palms along it and a path with red crushed brick, rather a pretty sight. There were a lot of dugout canoes tied up along the edges of the canal. They are well made and the natives handle them well. We passed a lumber yard where the natives were sawing the logs into boards by hand. The logs were set on trestles several feet off the ground and two men manned each saw; one on top of the log and another below. Quite a tedious way of making boards and planks I should think.

We noticed a lot of goats wandering about; fortunately they do not seem to have the same urge to bunt people as the goats at home have. In fact they pay no attention to people at all. Hens, roosters, chicks, ducks and geese wander everywhere about the streets of course.

Along some of the canal banks were many tons of sea shells. The natives burn them and so make lime. We watched them burning some at one place by putting it in a blacksmiths forge.

We saw three very pregnant women along a short space of road—all very proud of their condition as was quite obvious. The small boys continued to follow us, at intervals begging for bakshish and chanting that we were Babus (Indian Clerks) when we refused to give them any bakshish. To beg for bakshish is the first thing that a father teaches his son in this country. Indian children are invariably very bad mannered as little restraint is ever placed upon them.

There are hundreds of crows everywhere here and you can always hear their slow, lazy croaking. I suppose they help to keep the place clean. Generally speaking the houses here in Cochin seem to be larger and somewhat cleaner than in most Indian towns. The streets are made with red crushed brick and the houses roofed with red tile. The mate and I spotted a bird other than a crow in some bushes as we walked along and became quite excited about it. We stopped to watch a small boy fishing in a paddy field and as we watched as he caught a fish. He was in a great state of excitement over it and started to run away home to show it.

In the older part of the town there are many stone walls. Green moss seems to grow on everything here, the stone walls, the old houses and the old cathedral. It is the rainy season just now so it will have a good chance to grow. We noticed that a good share of the natives here are suffering from elephantiasis, a nasty looking skin disease where the skin thickens up until an arm or leg can hardly be recognized as such. It is supposed to be caused by drinking swamp water. As this is a very low-lying country around here and they have a lot of malaria as well.

We reached the jetty again; a good long walk and without any rain. We leave the jetty with the rickishaw wallas staring very accusingly at us. *"Truly the Sahibs must be mad to want to walk when they could easily have their bones thoroughly shaken in a fine rickishaw!"* they told us … and so back to the ship.

Our next port was Bombay and there Vickers was shifted to another ship much to everyone's regret. Lucas, Vickers and I always hit it off extremely well together and hate to see the crowd broken up—but such is life at sea. One day as I was entering the dock gates I bumped into Ginger Street. It had been over a year and a half since I saw him last so we had a lot to talk about. He came over the next day which was Sunday and he, Lucas and I went out to Breach Candy. This is a very nice swimming beach where only Europeans are admitted. Everything is pristine there with an indoor and outside swimming pool and chairs and tables all around. I noticed a lot of Jews there and I suppose that most of them are refugees. In the afternoon Lucas, Vickers and I went to see a football game at the Cooerage grounds. After that we had an hours billiards at the British India Club and then went out for dinner. After that we went to the pictures and then feeling that we had had a very full day we returned to the ship.

The Train to Kandy:

The next day as there was no work Lucas and I got around early and caught the train up to Kandy. First of all we passed through rice growing country where the natives were busy planting the young paddy plants. The big black water buffalo were pulling primitive looking wooden ploughs through the wet mud in just the same way as they did centuries ago. In other places they were pulling wooden scrappers over the fields to level them. Each small paddy field is surrounded by an earthen terrace so that the field can be flooded at will and there is a most complicated system of ditches for flooding them which I suppose have been developed through the centuries. At this time of the year (last of July) they are just sowing the rice itself by throwing it over the fields and working it into the soil. Later on when the young plants are partly grown the women and girls will have to transplant each paddy plant and that, I should think, must be about the last word in back-breaking labor.

The countryside looked luscious as we passed along. There were many palm trees of course and also many flowering shrubs and trees. The Singalese villages looked very clean with their palm thatched cottages and clean streets; much different from an Indian village. The stations we passed through often had very attractive names such as Ganemulle, Veyangoda, Ambepussa etc.

Gradually we traveled up into higher country and the scenery changed. The paddy fields were built up the sides of steep hills with their terraces making an odd pattern as we looked down at them. We began to see tea plantations and the little bushes looked very green against the red earth of the hillsides. In places we passed forests of rubber trees and could some-times see the slashes on the bark where they had been tapped for the precious latex.

(Singalese Robin Hood at Castle Rock)

We passed through a station called Anuradhapura, a junction station, and there I bought a large bunch of bananas for twenty five cents that kept us going for a long time. Soon we got into the really hilly country and it was an ever changing and beautiful sight as we climbed up into those hills. At times we had to have a push from another engine to get up some of the hills. In places you could look up at the mountaintops hundreds of feet above and in other places look an equal distance down. I t was all rather breath-taking. There was one large square mountain that we seemed to wind around many times and it is called Castle Rock. Apparently a robber used to hang out there during the middle of the last century and used to rob the stage coaches. Apparently he acquired a sort of reputation as a Singalese Robin Hood. Another well defined rock that we noticed several times is called Bible Rock and it looks like an open bible.

At Alagalla we had one of the finest views of the trip as we could see for miles down over the countryside. We came to a place called Sensation Corner where the tracks are laid along a narrow corner and you look down for a sheer drop of a thousand feet. The air was beginning to get cooler and we felt the change in atmosphere after so many months at sea level.

We noticed a tall white column at Kadugannawe that looked a bit too much like a lighthouse. We found afterwards that it was a memorial to a Captain Dawson who had built the road into the hills long before the railway was even thought of. At Peradeniya Junction we changed to another train and a few minutes after that we found ourselves at Kandy—we had arrived.

<u>The Temple of the Tooth:</u>

The first thing we did was to hire a taxi for the afternoon and then we went for a drive around the sacred lake which is near the center of Kandy.

Then we drove back to the Temple of the Tooth and started to look that over with the aid of a guide that we didn't want. There were a lot of stone carvings and the temple itself looked pretty ancient. The room that contained the sacred tooth of Buddha was heavily barred and I believe it is only taken out once a year or something like that when it is paraded about the town on the back of an elephant. Some of the stone carvings showed the Buddhist idea of Hell in a very realistic manner. There is apparently a special Hell for each special sort of sinner. A drunkard was shown being held down while boiling water was poured down his throat and other scenes in a like manner were quite abundant. There is a very old library in the temple of the Tooth containing many rare old Buddhist books and we had a look through that. The books are hundreds of years old and made of a certain kind of palm leaf. This leaf is about an inch and a half wide and perhaps a foot and a half long. The writing was done with a sharp piece of steel called a stylo and then ink smeared over the whole leaf and then wiped off leaving the ink in the scratches left by the stylo. Apparently this type of writing lasts a long time because those old books looked to be in pretty good shape. Many of them had precious jewels set in their covers. Some of them were said to be over a thousand years old and I suppose that is possible though it is quite a long time. This Temple of the Tooth had quite a history behind it though I cannot say as I was as impressed as I should have been. I have been rather spoiled by seeing so many fine Burmese temples which are always so much more picturesque.

Leaving the Temple of the Tooth we took the taxi out to a spot on the river called the "Elephants Bathing Pool". Here we saw over a dozen large and small elephants bathing and they certainly seemed to be enjoying themselves, especially when their mahouts were scrubbing them. I began to wish I had my camera but it is practically impossible for a sailor to take snaps now a days as the customs pounce on a camera like a dog on a rat.

We next went for a pleasant drive along the valley of the river and in due time arrived at the famous Peradeniya Gardens. The Gardens were a fine sight and the trees there were magnificent. We just wandered about and enjoyed it. The birds were singing and the flowers looked beautiful and I decided that if I ever had a day to spare in Colombo again I would just come up here to the Gardens for the afternoon. We had let the taxiwalla go but his mate had insisted on staying to show us around rather to our annoyance. He was rather amusing though for we saw some Boy Scouts teaching some Girl Guides how to ride bicycles and the guide very sadly told us *"thirty years ago white women learn to ride bicycle, now our women learning too, no good Master, no good."!* And he wandered along sadly shaking his head over the downfall of the modern Singalese girl.

We left the Gardens in time to walk the short distance to the Station and so caught our train back to Colombo again. We certainly had a fine day of it and it was a good change. We arrived in Colombo at about 9:30 pm.

Our next port was Madras and Lucas and I went out to the Technical Institute while there and bought a few curios. It is a nice ride out to Egmore Station via the electric train. At the Institute they have native handicrafts from all over Madras Presidency. I wasn't gong to buy anything but came away with a sandalwood carving of the Hindu God "Ganish" and he now adorns my desk. *(note … Alan's daughter, Mahrie, now owns this little carving)*

August 1941 (Rag-Chew in Calcutta)

We were back in Calcutta again around the first part of August, 1941. I met Smith at the depot, an old friend of mine. He is a quiet very distinguished looking gentleman who has been coming out on the coast for many years. We adjourned to Spence's Hotel, the common meeting ground for all the coastal "Sparks" and had quite a rag-chew"

On Saturday afternoon Smith and I went to the races and quite enjoyed ourselves. Then in the evening I took Lucas and wife to the pictures and had dinner at Firpos. They are going to Australia soon for his leave and he has already shifted from the ship to go on staff. I am really sorry to see him go as he is a grand chap and we have had some good times together.

Back in Bombay during the first of September. Went to a football match with Howarth one afternoon, then dinner at Monteinies and pictures. Our Chief Officer, Currie, has been transferred ashore as Assistant Cargo Superintendent. Our acting 2nd Davidson has gone up to C/O. Ironmonger is now the acting 2nd and we have an Iraqian 3rd Mate.

Our next port of call was Karachi. I bought some presents there for the folks at home. Karachi is about the best port for buying native handicrafts. Karachi is a bleak, barren sort of place populated by Indians and camels. It is built on the edge of a desert and consists mostly of sand and long distances. You are always pleasantly surprised when you see some green grass in Karachi.

September 1941 (Iran)

Bushire, Iran, was our next port of call. We anchored far off-shore as usual and unloaded into lighters. A more ragged, scruffy, sore-ridden bunch of cargo coolies I never saw than those Persians that came off. It was very hot there and the flies very persistent. On our way to the next port we managed to run aground as they had shifted a light; however we managed to get off without assistance and on our way again. Our talented 3rd Engineer wrote a poem, called *"Lost and Aground"*, about our little misadventure in the mud which I have included below.

Away off her course on Sunday night,
The poor Warina was in Hell of a plight;
But Monday noon a dhow was sighted,
Directions were given but our hopes were blighted,
For a mud bank nestling out of sight,
Drew us on, then held us tight:
the engineers then toiled and sweated,
but the mud held tight to what she'd netted;
But at two o'clock success was near,
Ahead, Astern, she's drifting clear;

And from the Bridge old Pop we hear,
Away lads, go and get some beer.
(29.9.41 by B.I. 3rd Engineer)

We arrived at Bandra Shapur, Iran, about the last of September with a cargo of wheat that had received much publicity in the papers as a present from the British Government to the poor starving Iranians who had sold all theirs to the Germans. Bandra Shapur proved to be a few buildings on the edge of a desert and boasted a water tank and a railway line. The water tank impresses me the most, partly because it was the highest thing in the place and partly because the old red duster was floating from above it as a sign of British occupation. There are quite a few sunken German ships in the harbor where they scuttled them as we occupied the place. I posted a couple of letters from the post office there but have grave doubts as to whether they will ever reach home as the Postmaster offered to accept cigarettes for the stamps.

Our next port was Abadan, Iran, one of the largest oil producing ports in the world. It is a weird looking place with huge tanks and miles of piping making a strange silhouette against the desert background. This is a very oily smelling place and I do not think I would care to live in this atmosphere along with the intense heat in the hot season. We have been fortunate enough to arrive here in the cool season and the weather is actually quite nippy at nights just now.

Palms:

We steamed up the *Shat-el-arab River* to *Basra* and it was a lovely sight as we pushed our way through the dead calm water with the sun going down like a great red ball of flame behind the date palms. I have been thinking what a marvelous tree the palm tree is because it supplies practically all the necessities of life for the natives. From the trunk they can make anything from building framework to canoe outriggers. The leaves can be used for thatching their huts and making mats to sit on. The buds can be tapped and from them is collected the milk that the natives make into that mildly intoxicating drink called toddy. The coconuts themselves can be cut open at almost anytime and a nice cool drink obtained from them. When they have matured the meat from the nut can be used for many things; oil can be obtained from it and it is good to eat both raw and cooked being very rich in food value. From the outside of the coconut is obtained the husk which can be woven into either ropes or mats. The shells themselves are often used as drinking cups so all told I don't suppose there is another tree in the world that is one quarter as useful as the ordinary coconut palm.

The *Shat-el-arabl River consists of* the combined waters of the *Tigris and the Euphrates*. Both banks of the river were covered with date palms and a greater percentage of the world's date crop comes from this portion of the world. We passed a lot of Arab dhows on the way up. They are amazingly seaworthy craft and capable of long sea journeys. There were several small villages along the river bank. The houses were square in design built of mud and with only small slits with no glass for windows. The wood smoke from the many evening fires drifted lazily over the river as the evening wore on and it smelled very fragrant. I noticed several flocks of pelicans flying along. They fly in a "V" formation the same as ducks and geese.

Mid October, 1941 … Bombay

We arrived back in Bombay about the middle of October. I met Fraser again at our Depot. We adjourned to the Grand Hotel where we had a good rag chew over drinks.

Mud Fish

Our next port was *Bhavnagar* and I must confess that I did not greet it with any enthusiasm. I went for a walk one evening and once again I noticed the many mud fish that seem to thrive on the mud when the tide goes out. They resemble what we call cat—fish at home. They walk over the mud by using their lower fins which are very stiff. They can hide themselves in an amazingly short time by burrowing into the soft mud.

We next called at Veraval and then at *Colombo*, after that we called at *Madras*. While I was at Madras I got a really pleasant surprise when a couple of fellows came over from another ship to see me about the B.W.M.S. Depot at Calcutta and they turned out to be Canadians off a Canadian ship. One was George Milne from Toronto and the other Gus Marshaldon from Midland. It was great to hear that good old Canadian drawl again and I hope to see them both at our next port.

At Calcutta I looked up George and Gus and showed them around a bit and greatly enjoyed doing it. I think I managed to show them most of the points of interest in Calcutta. We stayed in Calcutta several weeks while repairs were made to the ship and I stayed at the Marine Club.

Japan Enters the War (December 1941)

During this stay in port (December, 1941) Japan had suddenly entered the war. We called it treachery but as nearly everyone out here had been expecting them to do it, none of us could see what there was to be surprised about. The surprising thing is that they did not enter the war earlier! The Japs managed to sink two of our best warships, the *Prince of Wales* and the *Repulse* and that has altered the balance of power out here. The Japs have landed in *Malaya, Pearl Harbor* has been smashed up and the United States in now in the war. I'm afraid we are in for some pretty bad times around this way. There is little hope of getting much assistance from Britain out here just now as so many troops are tied up in Britain on account of the fear of invasion. Also with heavy fighting against the Germans and the Italians in the Middle East it also takes away a lot of our fighting strength out here. If the Americans cannot do something big out this way it looks as though we are in for a really rough time. Hong Kong is under a heavy siege just now and it appears as though it is just a matter of time until she has to pack up.

We spent Christmas day at sea but had a good dinner. They sent us away in a hurry at the last moment and we did not get into dry dock as we expected. The bottom plates are still covered with cement boxes to keep the water out, our propeller is half eaten away and looks ready to drop off, we haven't a gun of any description on board and are heading right into the war zone! The outlook isn't very bright. Our next port has already been heavily bombed we hear.

Dec. 27, 1941…. Rangoon

We arrived at Rangoon a couple of days after the Christmas day raid which was their second raid and a pretty heavy one. The air raid sirens were busy and we watched many dog-fights between the Japanese Zeros and the American "Flying Tigers". The Jap planes had bombed and machine-gunned the crowded streets and the results were heartbreaking. Around two thousand people were killed and the living departed into the jungle leaving a handful of Europeans, Anglo-Burmese and Anglo-Indians to clean up the mess. Rangoon was like a deserted ghost city when we arrived not a soul to be seen on the streets where formerly thousands had walked. Meals were left half eaten in houses and on street corners and patches of blood on the streets. They couldn't bury all the bodies so they had to throw many of them into the fires that were burning. The smell of half burnt, half decayed bodies floating out over the river each morning at breakfast time is just something I will not forget in a hurry.

Who ever would have thought three years ago that this peaceful happy country would be turned into a battle ground. What a pity it had to happen. There were no coolies of course so our cargo remained unloaded. We lay for days doing nothing off Latter Street Jetties. The stench from those half burned bodies was something terrific and even our Lascars were walking about with clothes around their faces. Small bands of people started to work digging them out for burial. At first there were quite a few bodies floating about in the river here but they have now disappeared, probably out to sea. The city was so silent both day and night that it was actually spooky. The RAF and AVG:s did good work during the raids and brought down about forty planes. The Jap bombs did not do so much damage to buildings as they were using anti-personnel bombs but they certainly damaged the people.

People gradually started to drift back into the city and we managed to get a few coolies who started work on our cargo. We hear that thousands of Indians here are attempting to walk overland to India. This is practically impossible as there are no actual roads and we hear that many of them are starving. Several shops were open again by the 31st of the month. As far as actual damage in the city here is concerned it is nothing as compared to what I saw in Britain. The English just carried on but here it is a different matter. There are so many thousands of ignorant people in these countries and no one has made any attempt to teach them anything about getting ready for war so this is just what one can expect.

It was New Year's day and the smell still hung about in the cabins. They are still digging out the remains from bombed sheds and warehouses. A few more Indians have returned but mighty few Burmese. They were keen enough on getting self-rule but do not seem to show up well in times like these. Troopships are coming in all the time but not enough of them. Many cargo vessels have to leave as there are no coolies to unload their cargoes … As the days passed by the Jap air attacks on Rangoon increased and we saw a lot of dog fights high over the city. The raids developed until the sirens seemed to be going both day and night. During this time I managed to acquire a bout of dengue fever which lasted ten days and didn't help me to enjoy things much.

Schiller was shifted to a local vessel running to Mergui just for that trip. In fact it was her last trip down there as they evacuated the place and brought refugees back with them. He then obtained leave and went over to Bassein with his wife to clear up her father's estate and then he re-joined us again. Some of us went up to the hospital and gave a pint of our blood. They needed it very badly and few volunteers were responding to their appeal for blood. *It was mostly the Merchant Service that was helping them out.*

When the air raids began the first people to beat it out of Rangoon were the Burmese Government people so I suppose we can hardly blame the poor ignorant coolies from coming back. From the way things have been going lately it looks as though any cargo unloaded would be for the Japs anyway.

January 14 1942 (War in the Pacific)

About the middle of January, 1942, they started bringing Burmese prison convicts on board to unload our cargo of coal as they were getting short of it ashore and the Indian coolies would not come back. The convicts seemed to enjoy the change although their work was pretty slow. Instead of the Government stepping in and forming labor battalions of the coolies they have done absolutely nothing. In fact the Burmese Government has proved to be worse than useless since Japan started her attacks. It is strange that the British military authorities have not taken things over.

Thai troops crossed the border on January 21st and there was heavy fighting in the Tenasserim district. Moulmein had been heavily bombed several times. On January 24th there was a heavy air battle near the city and our planes brought down twenty one enemy planes, five probables and nineteen damaged. We cannot see much in these fights as they are so high up but we can see the vapor trails winding in and out and hear the whine of the engines and the scream of the planes as they fell. The Japs are trying their best to blitz Rangoon again but our airmen can handle them. The air raid sirens never seem to cease.

There has been a lot of obstruction of cargoes here by customs red tape. No one seems to realize that there is a war on and that they, personally, will have to do something about it. Things have got so bad that the shipping companies are telling the Customs to go and get hanged, that there is a war on and that they will answer for anything afterwards if necessary. It certainly takes a lot to do away with red tape.

Part 6
War with Japan

o o o o o o o o o o o o o o o o o o o o o o o o o o o o o o o

The Moving Finger writes;
and, having writ,
Moves on: nor all thy Piety
nor Wit
Shall lure it back to cancel
half a line.
Nor all thy Tears wash out
a word of it.

(Rubaiyat of Omar Khayyam)

January 28th, 1942: The War with Japan

On January 28th our night fighters brought down a bomber over the city during the night. We saw the tracer bullets from our plane, the enemy plane burst into flame and then fall. The bombs exploded as it crashed and certainly lit things up. On January 29th there was another good air fight over the city and ten planes were brought down. Our planes—the RAF and the A"V G's can certainly look after the Japs.

Our troops had to fall back all the time. **Moulmein** was lost and the fight centered at Martaban for some time—just across the river from Moulmein. We did not have enough troops in the country to be of much use and what there were did not seem to be much good for jungle warfare. The Japs kept infiltrating behind them. Chinese troops were moving up but we had apparently turned down an offer of a strong enough force to be of some real use.

Heavy fighting was going on at **Martaba**n and at night we could see the gun-flashes reflected in the sky. Things looked bad and we began to wonder if we would be able to get our ship out to sea again or if we would be cut off. In fact I began to rather look forward to a trip up the Irrawaddy and perhaps through to China. They have been dropping quite a few bombs out near the ninth mile where Shriller and his wife and child have been staying and her nerves were getting a bit bad. Instead of moving her into the center of the city where she would be quite safe he had let her go up to Mandalay. Our argument was to keep her nearby as if we left in a hurry she might as well be on the ship or if we had to leave the ship and try to escape upcountry then we might as well be together but Shriller would not here of it. Mrs. Shriller, who is Burmese, remarked to me the other day that she was glad her face wasn't white. His little boy is also of a khaki hue. Shriller himself claims to be of Irish-German descent. He is also of very dark complexion.

Feb. 5th, 1942—from the Rangoon Gazette

"Now they are awake! The implications of the far Eastern war situation have not changed materially since Japan obtained naval command of the Pacific, and some of the possibilities in respect to Burma are very serious indeed. The fall of Moulmein must have opened the eyes of the blindest to reality. We are not daunted by possibilities and we know one certainty, that the defense of Rangoon, and the keeping open of the Burman Road, are so vital that they demand every effort and sacrifice, to the utmost limit of every single person's capacity; we know also people are willing and eager to answer all calls made upon them."

"People of Burma now being put to the test—any further withdrawal will be dangerous: We must stand and fight. If we fail now, our existence as a free nation if for ever doomed. We must take our courage and example from the Russian armies ... And, if we do have to go back, then let us be determined, as

were the Russians, to fight the Japanese on every inch of our soil, to the last shot, and, if necessary, to the last man. There were, however, some silver edges in an overcast sky, the Minister added. He spoke of the courageous conduct of Burmese troops during the battle of Moulmein, and of Burma engineers during the action on the routes from Kawkareik to the Salween. After referring to Mr. Churchill's promise of increasing reinforcements and to the valuable help we were receiving from China, the Minister said we might take heart from the recent actions of our American Allies."

We got hurried orders to get out as best we could on February 13th. Schiller had just sent his wife up to Mandalay so that did not help him. Quite a few ships had been sunk in the Bay by Jap subs and as I mentioned before we did not have a gun of any description on board. However, they had put a gun *platform* on our stern before we left so we built an imitation of a gun out of a mast spar and an empty oil drum. We hoped that if any sub saw it at a distance he might possibly mistake it for a gun and so prevent him surfacing and shelling us. I couldn't help thinking how futile and rather pathetic this was but still while there is life there is hope.

We had watched ships crowded with refugees leaving the port for days. It was a pathetic sight and we hoped that they would not be torpedoed for they were escorted. We had not seen any of the Royal Indian Navy during our forty five day stay in Rangoon. We had around eighty-four air raid warnings during this time and had got pretty fed up with them. Most of our cargo had been unloaded by the time we left—in time for the Japs—but we still had some left. We also found quite a few stowaways after leaving; mostly sampanwallas from Chittagong who just let their sampans float away and climbed on board.

During this stay in Rangoon both Hong Kong and Singapore had fallen and no wonder if they were run along the same lines as Rangoon. We have seen enough stupidity, blundering indifference and red tape during our forty-five day stay there to last a life time. I am sure that Rangoon will fall at the present rate and that seems to be the general opinion. We will not only lose Burma but India and Ceylon as well unless we can get some leaders out here quickly. These *old school tie wallas* have not shown up very well out this way. The only way that Rangoon can be held is to keep the seaway open and they do not seem to be doing that. **We saw no patrol ships at all while at sea, the poor old Merchant Service has to just plug along on its own with no protection and no guns.**

We arrived in Calcutta safely—thanks to no one but ourselves. Schiller, who is Gunnery Officer when we have any guns, went up to the Royal Indian Navy and told them we wanted some guns before sailing. They had the cheek to turn around and say they had no time to arm us and when Schiller said that the general atmosphere was that no one would sail without a gun they said *"Don't you know there is a war on you can't hold up the ship"*. So they were told that they were the ones that would be holding the ship up. We got our guns. The general attitude of the people here in Calcutta is one of complete indifference to the war. **They hate the sight of the Merchant Service** as much as ever and they can't go to enough trouble to make trouble for us whenever possible. It is likely that only a good bombing could do them any good and make them realize that this war is a grim and terrible business.

Our next port was **Trincomalee**, a beautiful spot on the east side of Ceylon that I have mentioned before. Rangoon fell during the first part of March and the Japs seized the Anderman Islands. We had heavy fleet losses in the battle of the Java sea and things seemed to be going from bad to worse all over the place.

March 13th, 1942: Trincomalee, Ceylon (From Bad to Worse)

We arrived here some days ago. We are a *Merchant Fleet Auxiliary* and it looks as though we are in for a long and weary stay here. This is my second visit to this port. It is one of the deepest and finest harbors in the world but has never been developed. There is a small village here with natural scenery and Palm groves and jungle.

On April 7th, 1942

Colombo had a heavy air raid but the attackers were beaten off with heavy losses. Twenty-seven enemy planes shot down and possibly as many damaged. They must have been from aircraft carriers as the nearest land is about seven hundred miles away. It was a bang up raid while it lasted and we were lucky to not have suffered too many losses.

Then on the morning of April 9th they attacked **Trincomalee** and believe me it was a hot time while it lasted. I was awakened by the scream of shells and thought we were being bombarded from the sea. Grabbing my tin helmet I rushed into the alleyway and asked a couple of cunnies what was up. They pointed upwards and said *"hawa jhaz"* so I knew it was planes. I didn't see any of the other officers about so dashed up to the bridge amidst thunderous explosions. I found everyone just sticking their heads out of the wheel house where they had taken cover. All hell seemed to have broken loose about us and I wondered if this were the beginning of the invasion. The Jap planes were flying high, far out of range of our machine guns, and they never broke formation (the bombers) despite the terrific barrage that was being put up by our battleship. Their bombing was very accurate despite their height. As we had a ten thousand ton supply ship on one side of us and a dredger on the other we must have been the best target in the port. Every time we saw some bombs leave those planes we thought sure they were for us. Some of them came fairly close and a ship near us was hit but we came through it safely. Quite a few bombs landed in the water nearby. It was some half hour while it lasted and we were surely glad when it was over. It was a very heavy raid and the Japs seemed to get nearly everything they have wanted on the shore. It was a dead calm morning and when the bombs hit the smoke rose lazily in the air for several hundred feet. It was rather a weird sight amidst the setting of tropical beauty. We did not see any Jap planes brought down but heard later that they had lost several. I heard that ten ships were sunk in the Bay Sunday night including my old ship. (*The S/S Indora*) The Jap fleet or part of it is apparently around here. **Where is our navy?** We also heard that about forty Jap transports laden with invasion troops that were hanging off Ceylon had turned back to Rangoon. After the raid Trincomalee was deserted as all the natives beetled off into the jungle as per usual. All ships except ourselves and a few small ones left the place and they were shifting most of the naval stuff out of the place. In fact it looked as though we were going to abandon Trincomalee if there was any trouble. We wonder if the Japs are trying an invasion here. Several coastal ports in India have been bombed.

April 9th, 1942: (Air raid at Trincomalee, Ceylon)

We had a rather terrific air raid here this morning. We were bombed and strafed by Japanese bombers and zeros. Bombers dropped heavy bombs from a high attitude but did not hit us. We put up a terrific barrage around here but **where were our planes?** We lost ten merchant ships, two cruisers, the Dorsetshire and the Cornwall and an aircraft carrier (*The Hermes*) in the Bay of Bengal. The HMS moniter *"Arabus"* was badly damaged and many sailors dead and wounded. They got the ship lying ahead of us and they had to beach her. Things are going badly for us.

Between four and five hundred survivors from Merchant ships landed in India. We heard that there were over fifty to sixty Japanese planes over here the other day. Their bombing was quite accurate and the bomb craters were over thirty to forty feet deep and sixty feet wide. They must be our own Singapore bombs. Almost all the natives here have fled this place and no shops are open and the market is closed so we are living one tin to the next. One of the most discouraging things of war is the lack of support from the people themselves. We are wondering if we will ever get out of here. The Japs seem to have the upper hand in the Bay of Bengal at the moment and if they stage an invasion this will be one hot spot. We do not have the necessary men or material out here.

April 15th, 1942: Trincomalee, Ceylon

During a heavy raid the other day a ship right near us was hit by bombs. The ship had to be beached and then it burned out. Other vital navy places were struck. It was some blitz! On a happier note I received some mail from home today for the first time since coming here and I certainly was glad to get it. We went ashore for the afternoon to see that many of the natives had returned. I suppose they were getting hungry in the jungle. **We are apparently known as a Merchant Fleet (auxiliary now)** I sure hope they get some more planes around here before there is another raid. It seemed a a bit pathetic last time.

April 19th, 1942 (Trincomaleee, Ceylon—M.F.A. Warina)

The tropical beauty around here is beginning to pall on us. The weather is hot both day and night. If wishes were horses we would surely be out of this port. All of us are tired of it and it is like being buried alive on top of a volcano. We have had no ice in some time now and surely miss it in this hot climate. For about a week after the last raid we could get no potatoes and had to live on beans. There are fish in the harbor here but they seem hard to catch.

My swimming has improved almost beyond recognition since coming here. Sometimes we go out three and four times a day. The days seem to drag here and I'm sure we will never get rid of our cargo at this rate. I would like to be at sea again whatever its dangers might be. We all wish that things would go a bit better for us in Burma because we are all fully convinced that Ceylon will be their next objective if Burma falls.

April 29th, 1942—Trincomalee, Ceylon

We are having a bit of trouble in getting the "Old Man" to put out his lights up there at night. We have all told him about it too. No use of us dimming our lights and keeping blackout if his deck is in a glare of light.

Our Wooden Gun!

Gun Crew
S/S Indora

Just Me!
(Alan K M. Patterson)

April 30th, 1942 Trincomalee, Ceylon

It looks as though we are doomed to be the last ship here no matter what happens. We will be about the only target in the port if we get another air raid. Our ship's Agent never returned after the raid, neither has the ship's chandler so it means we have to scrounge around every day for meat and vegetables and we have to row or sail ashore to do so.

May 6th, 1942

Air raid sirens went this morning and a lot of our planes are about but we saw nothing else. We moved the guns of course and were all set for trouble We are in a bad spot here and stand little chance if trouble comes.

May 7th, 1942

They were firing the anti-aircraft guns today and gave us no warning so we thought at first it was a real raid. Apparently yesterday' s raid was practice as well though we were not told about it.

May 8th, 1942—The Welsh "Sparks" from a naval ship was on board tonight. We are quite popular because we have beer on board but we can always raise some tobacco from them in return.

May 31st, 1942—Trincomalee, Ceylon

Today we shifted from the wreck of the Sagong to a spot near the Town Jetty. It would be very handy if the monsoon were not blowing so hard. It is too strong for the ship's Jolly boat. We have a southwest monsoon gale and it is quite rough even in the Bay here. A Motor-launch has been taking the Butler ashore for provisions these past few days.

June 3, 1942

I'm afraid things are not what they might be on here. Our old man—a two hundred pounder—does not interest himself in the ship much and is plainly being carried by the mate who is very conscientious.

June 8th, 1942—Capt. Johnson has arrived to relieve Captain Drummond today. I have sailed with him before on my last ship and he is a most efficient ship-master. His last ship was sunk by Japs in the Bay.

June 9th, 1942

I went ashore this morning to send a cable home. First we have to get them censored at the Naval Office and then go the post office to send them.

June 12th, 1942: Our food has improved considerably on here with the arrival of our new Captain. We have fresh fish for a change now. I hope never to see a tinned herring again.

Ginger Street, Kew,
Alan Patterson
S.S. Indora

Attwater 4th Eng.
S.S. Indora

Schiller-Bramal
Captain Johnson
S.S. Warina

Painting the stack!

Schiller - Patterson
S/S/ Warina

Alan Patterson- 1938

1st Mate S/S Marslew on left
R/O Patterson on right.

3rd Officer Turk -1940

2nd Officer Kew
S.S Indora

June 14th, 1942—The Times of Ceylon

"Marine's Guerrilla Epic In Burma—Free Lance Mission Against Odds—volunteered for an unknown mission, were hunted by the Japanese day and night, fought against heavy odds inflicting severe casualties, underwent difficulties never before experienced, and helped to evacuate an army. This briefly, is the proud and creditable record of a band of daring, dashing royal Marines who risked their lives for their King and Empire in the recent Burma campaign and who are now with us in Ceylon."

June 23rd, 1942:

Trincomalee, Ceylon: Our troops have lost a lot of ground in Libya. Tobruck has fallen and things seem to be in a rather bad way generally in the Middle East. The German troops are only a hundred miles from the Egyptian border. It will be bad for us if they gain control of the Suez Canal. Apparently people are pretty much upset about our losses in the Middle East now and demand an investigation. They should have started long ago with Brooke-Poppen of Singapore fame.

June 25th, 1942—The Duke of Gloucester was here today and redirected the troops etc. Quite a bit of excitement ashore here.

<u>July 10th, 1942—S.S. Warina at Sea!!!</u>

Finally at sea again. The sea is smooth and it is good to be on the go again. There are many Jap subs and battleships around here. Quite a few of us will sleep close to our life jackets until we reach our next port.

July 12, 1942—Colombo, Ceylon: We had a fairly rough trip, but here we are safe and sound. Will likely go ashore tomorrow for a look around.

July 18th, 1942—Columbus:

Attended a lecture at D.E.M.S this morning on Marlin Machine guns and another on anti-aircraft guns. I'm concentrating on the anti-aircraft gunnery lessons as that is all I will ever have a chance to use.

July 26th, 1942—Warina at sea.

July 29th, 1942-still at sea and going around in circles. We are quite dizzy from it. We do see things but its quite pathetic.

August 3rd, 1942—At sea—Its rather a tense atmosphere here in the Bay of Bengal now. Every fish that jumps looks like a periscope and there are enemy planes and warships to be watched for. *It would be nice to see some of the famous Royal India Navy—where are they?*

August 10th, 1942—Calcutta

Here we are safe and sound and nothing exciting during the voyage but with no thanks to anyone but ourselves and our luck.

August 20th, 1942—S/S Warina—at sea

A ship just twenty miles away from us got bombed today. Enemy bombers must have seen us at that distance but he must have been out of bombs. We thought we were for it but its been our lucky day.

August 24th—Trincomalee, Ceylon

Here we are again all set for another siege of isolation and monotony. After over five months here last spell and now due for the same again I'm afraid we will all be pretty fed up with it by the end of our time here.

September 17th, 1942—Trincomalee: This is some isolated life here. What there is of the Naval crowd here seem to be such a gin-sodden bunch that none of us have any wish to get too friendly with them. So we stick to ourselves horrible as that may be.

October 18th, 1942—Trincomalee, Ceylon

A hard day today. All the officers went down to the hold and worked with the engineers to get the job finished so they could get away and help a ship in trouble. There was a call to rescue men from a ship in the Bay. Later our officers received praise for a job well done.

November 8th, 1942—At Sea (S/S Warina

It is mighty nice to be at sea again despite its additional dangers. The sea is calm with a heavy swell and some showers. No subs have been reported close at hand yet anyway. It is surely great to be on watch again. Never thought I could grow as tired of just doing nothing.

November 10th—Adder Atoll, Maldive Islands

We are anchored in a lagoon off a coral Island. It is low lying and covered with palm trees. We are just a few miles south of the equator and Indian Ocean. There is nothing to do ashore here, this is a very lovely spot and unheard of in peace-time. There is a lot of malaria among troops ashore here. It rains quite steadily and it seems an unhealthy sort of steamy climate. I saw some Maldive Islanders today. They wear queer shaped black hats, black coats and leggings. They are good sailors.

December 8th, 1942—Trincomalee, Ceylon—back to our old port.

December 23rd, 1942—S/S Warina—at sea again in submarine infested waters. Hope our luck will hold. I'm all alone so I guess I'll do a few extra watches.

December 24th, 1942—We are rolling along in the Bay of Bengal. We are all alone as usual. I often wonder where the Royal Indian Navy hang out. We certainly don't see much of them afloat.

December 25th, 1942—Another Christmas day at sea. Beyond eating a bit more than usual it has been the same as any other day at sea for us.

Dec. 27, 1942 (A Marconi gram sent by the Admiralty)

"BAMS7A—FROM ADMIRALTY

THE FOLLOWING IS A MESSAGE ADDRESSED TO ALL SHIPS OF THE UNITED NATIONS FROM THE BRITISH MINISTER OF WAR TRANSPORT STOP AS MINISTER OF WAR TRANSPORT I SEND TO ALL SEAMEN OF THE UNITED NATIONS AT THIS CHRISTMAS MY WARMEST GREETINGS AND BEST WISHES ON BEHALF OF THE BRITISH PEOPLE STOP WE REALIZE TO THE FULL THE HARDSHIPS AND PERILS OF OUR WORK STOP WE ADMIRE OUR ENDURANCES AND COURAGE AND WE KNOW HOW MUCH GREATER THE VICTORY WE ARE GOING TO WIN WILL BE DUE TO YOU STOP GOOD LUCK TO YOU ALL STOP"
"Message taken by Ship's Radio officer AKMP"

New Years Day, 1943

Here we are back in Calcutta. We arrived shortly after a small Japanese air raid. The place now seems almost empty. Where are all those seething, shouting, betel nut chewing mobs of Indians that usually swarm along Calcutta's streets? Surely a few little fifty pound anti-personal bombs has not had this startling effect! What would a real raid do I wonder. Apparently the railway station was mobbed after this raid. Thousands and thousands of our brave (?) Bengali's poured out of the city by rail and road. Babies and coolies forgot caste and creed in their own blind rush to get out of the city. The streets seem strangely silent, taxis are scarce and very costly, tram services are almost stopped, garbage has not been collected from city street corners for days and the city smells even worse than usual. We had to get into dry dock as best we could without any help as the labor has fled. In other words if the Japs make a small raid here once in a while the story of Rangoon will repeat itself. The River is silting up rapidly as the dredger coolies have fled so shipping will cease in time if they do not get going. The air force and army are strong here now compared to Rangoon but if the Indian labor runs away every time it will create a problem. Only time can tell how things will end.

July 1943: Trincomalee, Ceylon:

It is well over a year since the big Japanese air raid. We do not stay here so long now and sometimes go to a coral island out in the Indian Ocean. In my opinion coral islands are not what they are cracked up to be. On our first trip down there scrub-typhus was raging and men were dying off like flies. Now with the clearing of the island they seem to have it more or less under control. I don't think they ever found out for sure just what caused it but it seemed to be mostly men who were at work clearing scrub that caught it. If you cut your leg or arm there you have to be careful or the first thing you know a coral ulcer has started. The only consolation when we visit that place is the good fishing and the coral reef that rings the inside of the vast lagoon as well as around the outside of each island. On a calm day it is a magnificent sight to look down into the coral reef from a boat. All sorts of fantastic and beautiful corals and fishes are seen below. It is quite breath taking in its beauty and not a sight to be missed. We did a lot of fishing here in Trinco and and a lot of sailing in both places. It helps fill in the time very nicely. It is a pretty monotonous job. We are usually only in Calcutta for a few days and then for several months at a time we are cooped up together here with no place to escape to. We get so that we know exactly what the other person is going to say and all those annoying little mannerisms that show up like sore thumbs. However we just have to make the best of it and it is really surprising how well we do get along despite everything. There have been some changes on ship during the year to add a bit of variety. Handcock was relieved by Murphy who in time was relieved by Cockeroft. Schiller our 2nd officer left the ship here at Trinco a few weeks ago, he was found to be suffering from TB. Have heard from him and apparently they have caught it in time and hope to patch him up again in a few months. He was certainly a very strong character and a very different from the rest of us in his way of thinking. He was the most boastful little man I have ever met and never lost a single opportunity to tell you what a fine fellow he was. However he was a very good hearted chap and would certainly go to no end of trouble to help anyone out. He has been relieved by Boweran who will soon be going up for his Master's ticket. Captain Johnson who joined us last June, is still here. I sailed with him on the *S.S. Indora* and seem to have spent nearly half my time at sea sailing with him.

July 19, 1943. Ceylon

The Sirens wailed and we manned our guns in the early hours of the morning. It was brilliant moonlight almost like day. We saw no enemy planes but gunfire was fairly close. No doubt Japs are anxious to find out all about Trincomalee since their last visit.

September 21, 1943 *(Starvation in Bengal from "The Times of Ceylon")*

Reports Keep Coming In of Daily Deaths From Hunger—Calcutta
While strenuous measures to meet the food situation in Bengal are continuing, reports keep coming in daily of deaths due to starvation in the streets of Calcutta and other towns of Bengal. According to the British-owned Calcutta paper "The Statesman" which publishes statistics, the publicly recorded number of bodies disposed of in Calcutta by various organizations from August 1st to September 15 totals over 2,100. In addition, the total admissions to hospitals between August 16 and September 16 are over 3,500. (Associated Press)
__London Comments:__ *This weeks "New Statesman" makes the following comment on the Indian famine: "The news of the Indian famine is still so terrible that our imaginations shrinks from the task of picturing it." "While we think that the Muslim league's Coalition Ministry in Bengal is unequal to its responsibilities, the major blame falls on the Center which clung until the other day to a doctrinaire policy of free trade in food. The paper adds that the crisis goes further than shortage of rice. It is all one economic problem and we look to Lord Wavell to change the atmosphere but things have to be done on a mass scale> "*

October, 1943 (Calcutta)

There is quite a famine here now. Supplies of rice have been cut off from Burma and of course the cyclone that swept up the Houghli delta last November destroyed a lot of the rice crop and to make matters worse many Indians have been hoarding the rice and making huge profits. Indians have self government in the province of Bengal here and they have been so busy passing motions and exploring every avenue and forming committees and sub-committees that they have paid little attention to the famine that was starting last March. They had to buy some wheat from one of the other provinces eventually but were too busy selling it at a profit for the starving people to see any of it. This famine is not a thing that an individual can do much about unless he has the power to get others doing something about it as well. It is a case where millions of starving people are involved and they are picking the dead off the streets each day here. I have seen many poor souls digging in dust bins for scraps. They have started soup-kitchens in some parts of the city and the people are lined up for blocks waiting their turn. Even in prosperous times so many of these people live on the borderline of absolute poverty that it does not take much to trip the balance in the wrong direction.

Bengal is the province from whence much future action against the Japs will take place so the Central Government has been very foolish not to step in long ago and so prevent this situation from developing as it is bound to impede the war effort. Prices have risen by almost 500 percent here on many things and there is profiteering everywhere. There is bound to be an epidemic of some kind here with all these starving people and this city so filthy. Refuse lies on the streets for days here and the smells are horrible.

November/December 1943 (Trincomalea, Ceylon)

The month of November we had the most marvelous fishing up here in Cod Bay. The fish are called "Butter fish" here locally. They are shaped like a salmon but silver in color. They were about three feet long and weighed up to fifteen pounds. Captain Johnson, Blair and I used to row over near the beach every morning and fish and we enjoyed some of the finest fishing I have ever experienced. Every fish fought like something gone mad. They leaped out of the water and shook their heads, tried to run for the mangrove roots near the shore and in fact tried every trick a fish knows when hooked. Our best catch was thirteen in one morning counting several millet. The total catch weighed sixty six pounds.

When the fish were not biting it was good fun just to watch the monkeys swaying through the trees in the jungle along the edge of the water and to listen to the numerous jungle birds. The scenery is really beautiful around here just now as the rains have freshened everything up and the leaves on the trees look very green. There is one bird in particular whose song we noticed and it sounded like a thrush. There are a couple of large black and white sea eagles that soar around here as well and they look quite majestic. The sailing has been good between rains and we have had some good times. We missed this nice season here last year as we were on the Maldive ring.

We heard over the radio that Calcutta now has bad cholera epidemics with thousands dying. That is not in the least surprising as anyone with any common sense could see what was coming if they did not clean the place up a bit.

Dec. 31st, 1943 (At sea)

Here we are rolling around at sea. There is half an hour to go before midnight and 1944 rolls in! My Junior, Blair, will be coming on watch at midnight. He is from Dundee and this is his first Hognany spent at sea. (I think that is the way the Scotchmen spell it) Well, we have been through some pretty hard years since this war started and I suppose this coming year will see the hardest fighting of all both on land and sea. Things are warming up again out here in the Bay once more. This is the first real convoy I have been in along the Indian coast. Once in a while we have had a solitary escort vessel to ourselves if it happened to be going our way but that is all! We have been very lucky as we have plowed up and down the coast unharmed while many a better ship than ours has gone down by enemy action. The night before we left Trincomalee I was over on one of the bar boats to say goodbye to Skipper Buchan as he is going home on leave. I will miss him. He and Paddy O'Rourke the Chief Engineer are the two old timers of the place. Their ship, another loan defense vessel, ourselves and a tug were all that was left there when the Japs were expected at any moment. Those were grim days and we have seen some changes since then. I'll miss Buchan very much. He is a typical Scotch trawler skipper, ruddy complexion, stubborn, character enough for a dozen men and a man you could always trust. He is one of the best types I have met. He and O'Rourke make a good combination and they swear by each other—when the other one isn't around! I have met and worked with many many good men since signing on as Ship's Radio Man back in 1938. Below is a poem written by one of our brave men about our Merchant Marine Service men and how under appreciated they are by the public.

The Merchant Service Bum:

You've seen him on the street,
Rolling round on groggy feet;
You've despised him when he's been out on a spree. But you didn't see the trip
On a dark and lonely ship
Through a submarine and mine infested sea.

You have cheered the navy lads
On their heavy ironclads;
You can spare a cheer for tommy Atkins too.
You may have a touch of funk
When you read "Big mail boat sunk",
did you think of the merchant service crew?

You have mourned about the cost
Of every vessel lost-
It has put you in a pessimistic mood.
But you never said "Well done!"
Or congratulated one,
Who helps to bring your wife and kiddies food.

He has brought your wounded home
through a mine infested zone;
He has ferried all your troops to France by night.
He belongs to no brigade,
Is neglected, underpaid—
yet is often in the thickest of the fight.

He has fought the lurking hun
With an ancient four inch gun;
And he's done his bit to get them on the run.
Yet you've never heard him boast
to the folks that need him most....
In fact he's rather reticent and glum.

Wouldn't you feel that way too,
If, no matter what you do,
You're still another merchant service bum"
He can collar huns and smite'em
To the real "Ad infinitum'"
And as for wops he doesn't give a damn.
His social standing's nil,
You regard him as a pill,
But you've got to hand it to him.... He's a man.

Written by one of us who has since lost his life by enemy action.
A hero, unsung but not forgotten.

Part 7
Darjeeling and a Glimpse of Everest

○ ○

Alas, that Spring should
vanish with the Rose!
That Youth's sweet-scented
Manuscript should close!
The Nightingale that in the
Branches sang,
Ah, whence, and whither
flown again, who knows?

(Rubaiyat of Omar Khayyam)

Calcutta, India

Calcutta, even at the beginning of the hot season, is not a nice city to live in. During the first few days we had suffered from the sultry overpowering heat, the dust, the ever shrieking coolies and the millions of hard-biting mosquitoes. We thought that we would be sailing but orders were suddenly changed and we learned that we would be staying in Calcutta for twelve days or so. I also found that I would have to shift out of my cabin while repairs were being made. By this time I was quite fed up with Calcutta so I asked Captain Johnson for seven days leave to go up to Darjeeling. The leave was willingly granted. Captain Johnson helped me get the railway tickets through the ship's agents, telegraphed friends of his in Darjeeling that I was leaving that night and asked them to secure accommodations for me when I arrived. He helped me in every way possible and I will always remember his kindness.

I left Calcutta at night from Sealdah Station by the Darjeeling mail train. One of the Babbus from the agent's office had been sent along to secure my berth and the 2nd Officer turned up just before we left to see me off. I had a first Class compartment and two army officers for traveling companions. It is three hundred and eighty six miles from Calcutta to Darjeeling and the monotonous part of the journey over the plains is covered during the night. After securely locking the doors to prevent our baggage being stolen during the night we turned in. Train travel is a bit different in India than in most countries. You have to carry your own bedding, soap, etc. Fortunately I had heard about that before and was prepared for it. Also the tickets are merely checked at both ends of the journey. That method is so efficient that I still have my "up" portion of the ticket as a souvenir of the journey.

We reached Siliguri in the morning and that is as far as the Darjeeling mail goes. I had breakfast at the station and then changed over to the Darjeeling Himalayan Hill Railway. It looked like a toy railway with its little engine and small coaches running on rails that could not have been over two feet apart. I noticed that the engine-driver fireman and brakemen were all Nepalese and I saw quite a few around the station. Their features were all distinctly Mongolian and they looked to be very sturdy little men.

We left Siliguri and soon were passing through heavily wooded country along the foothills of the Himalayas. The hunting is good in that region and there are plenty of wild elephants, buffaloes, bears, tigers and many other animals. We continued to climb and as we went up the forest became thinner and the views more magnificent. The railway line followed the edge of the cliff most of the time and we could look out and down into sheer space. The grade was very steep at times and we could hear the engine wheels skidding. I thought of that very small engine and wondered if it would make the grade. We climbed until we came to a complete loop in the line and passed right over the track below. I saw then that there were a couple of men standing on the front of the engine throwing sand on the rails to prevent the wheels from skidding too much. I wondered if those fellows were known as sandmen. We went around three loops as we climbed. These apparently serve to lessen the gradient. On reaching the third loop we were about 2,000 feet above sea level. The countryside and the people were both changing. We were getting away from the dark complexioned peace loving Bengali and it was good to see the smiling, good looking Mountaineers. Many of these had quite fair complexions and many of the women and children had rosy cheeks. We began to see pine trees, the first I had seen for a long time and they looked good to me. Most of these people farm their little hillside farms and that must be some job as they consist of terraces built along the sides of the steep hills. Few of these mountaineers have much wealth but they are a happy and independent people: their women enjoy a freedom quite unknown to the women of the plains; apparently they do most of the work as well. We passed many tea estates with the green tea shrubs covering the many hills.

The little engine puffed and snorted up the mountainsides, the sandmen threw sand upon the rails as the wheels skidded, the wheels of our carriages moaned and screamed as we made sharp bends in the track and I wondered if we would actually make it. Then the train stopped and we started backing up a hill; we backed up to a fairly level spot and then started going ahead again. Apparently this is yet another way of overcoming a very steep gradient. We came to a couple more of these zigzags before we reached the top. We climbed to 4,000 feet and then to 5000 feet. Far below us we could see valleys and rivers and in the distance the plains of Bengal. The train continued to climb until we reached Ghoom which is 7,407 feet above sea level. We had passed through banks of cloud at about 5,000 feet and from Ghoom it was like looking down on another world. From Ghoom we descended some six hundred feet and were soon at our destination. I had not worn my uniform but when the train stopped the Captain's friends, Mr. And Mrs. Bee, walked right up to me through the crowds and asked if I were Mr. Patterson so I suppose a sailor's beard has its uses. Mrs. Bee runs the New Elgin Hotel for her sister and they had a room for me. I had to share it with a Flight Lieutenant as the place was crowded. He turned out to be a grand fellow and I only hope it will be my good fortune to meet him again some day.

That night Mr. And Mrs. Bee took us to the Gymkhana Club and the Flight Lieutenant and we became temporary members for our stay there. It is one of the bright spots in Darjeeling with dances three times a week, three bars, a billiard room, skating rink, tennis courts and the opportunity to meet many people. We made good use of it all the time I was there. I met so many people that I couldn't hope to remember their names and it was a great change from shipboard life.

The next morning the four of us went for a walk around the Mall before breakfast. It is about the only fairly level road in Darjeeling. The air was cold and sparklingly clear. We rounded a bend in the road and there before us was one of the most magnificent views I have ever seen in my life. Kinchenjunga, second highest mountain range in the world, seemed to tower over us. It was covered with snow, the first I had seen for several years. Words cannot described its beauty and no camera or painting could ever hope to do it full justice. We could see other mountain ranges in the distance but Kinchenjunga completely overshadowed all. Looking down through the clouds we could see peaceful little valleys and winding rivers thousands of feet below. It all went to make up such an awe-inspiring and beautiful scene that it took a great effort to tear myself away from it to follow the others back to the hotel—and breakfast.

The weather was very chilly at Darjeeling. To me it felt mighty cold after so long on the Indian Coast. I had to keep on the move just for the sake of keeping warm. My first try at climbing a hill left me gasping for breath after the first few feet. I was not used to such a rarefied air and found that I had to climb hills very slowly for the first few days until I became used to it. Every place you go in Darjeeling seems to be either up or down hill.

The houses are nearly all built on cliffs, or rather on the edges of them. It would not do to be a sleep-walker in Darjeeling—if you stepped out a window it would probably result in quite a fall. The only method of getting about besides walking is by taxi or rickshaw. It takes four sturdy mountaineers to propel a rickshaw: two pulling and two pushing and even then they certainly have to work for a living.

Sunday was market day so after breakfast we wandered down to the market to have a look at the people. What a happy, cheery crowd they appeared to be as compared to a Calcutta market. Most of the men wore caps trimmed with fur. The women, many of them carrying babies on their backs, seemed to be taking an active part in the buying and selling. Many of them wore large shell-like necklaces and many wore some sort of ornament fastened to their noses. There were several different types of natives; some came from Nepal, some from Sikkim and others from Bhutan. All of these are independent states and the mountain ranges of all their borders can be seen from the Observatory Hill, at the base of which runs the Mall Road. It is from Nepal that the Indian Army gets its finest fighting men—the Gurkhas. They are sturdy good natured little men with Mongolian features: good natured, that is, until it comes to a fight and then they take a lot of stopping.

Early the next morning the Flight Lieutenant and I crawled out of our nice warm beds into the cold and darkness of five o'clock and took a car out to Ghoom, about six miles from Darjeeling, and so on to Tiger hill. The road was very steep and nothing but a small car could have got around the steep and very sharp corners. We had to get out of the car and climb the last half mile on foot. It was such a steep and hard climb that it seemed more like ten miles by the time we reached its peak. There were already several other people there shivering in the frosty atmosphere of 8,515 feet and patiently waiting for the sun to rise.

Gradually the horizon brightened and we could see the glow of the snows of the mighty **Kinchenjunga** range. Then other peaks became visible and we just had a glimpse of the very peak of **Mount Everest** before the clouds, which had been steadily rising from below, cut off our view and we were left standing in the swirling mists. **Mount Everest** is 29,002 feet high but as it is nearly one hundred and seven miles away from Tiger Hill it is quite overshadowed by the near-by Kinchenjuga range. It is 28,225 feet high and so is second in height to Mount Everest. These are of course the most famous mountains but all around are mountain ranges. To the west lies the Singalila range of mountains that mark the boundary between Nepal and Sikkim. Truly this is a land of mountains, valleys and rivers. The scenery is almost overpowering in its magnificence. The ever changing coloring of the mountain peaks is impossible to describe and one has to actually see it to begin to appreciate it.

The remainder of my stay at Darjeeling was mostly spent in sight-seeing about the town, admiring the ever beautiful scenery, and trying to keep warm by means of vigorous exercise and wearing all available clothing. One morning the Flight Lieutenant and I hired a couple of mountain ponies and rode a few times around the Mall. We chose that for our ride as it seemed to us to be about the only place where we might not have to fall a few thousand feet if we tumbled off the ponies. Fortunately for us the ponies could not be stirred into making more than a few half hearted attempts to trot so we did not fall off.

We spent one night out at Keventers farm near Ghoom. Mr. Bee is the manager and we had an interesting time looking over what is no doubt one of the highest farms in the world. They keep about two hundred dairy cattle and hundreds of pigs. The milk is pasteurized on the spot, some of it is made into cheese and butter is also made. They cure their own hams and bacons and make sausages. Most of the buildings are built on the edge of cliffs and it seemed to me that mountain goats would be more suitable for that spot. All the fodder for the cattle has to be brought up from the plains. It looked as though farming at a height of 7,407 feet must take a lot of planning.

My holiday ended all too rapidly and it was with regret that I climbed into the little mountain train again to return to the heat of the plains. It had been a great change in every way especially the scenery and the hospitable people that I met, both quite unlike the coast in every way. I left Darjeeling in the afternoon and fully enjoyed the scenery on the way down. It was dark when we reached Siliguri and changed over to the large train. We arrived back at Sealdah Station, Calcutta, early the next morning ... And so back to the ship once again....

January 1, 1944—November 1945

We continued to follow the Royal Naval Ships around. We mostly traveled between the Naval port of Trincomalee on the east coast of Ceylon and Addu Atoll in the Maldive Islands. I continued to serve on the **S/S Warina** until the 23 July 1944 when I joined the **S/S Samspring** homeward bound to the U.K. By then the Suez Canal had been cleared and it was a much shorter voyage than around by Africa.

We had to creep through the Straits of Dover by night as the Germans still had their big guns on the Coast of France. On arriving in the Port of London, I was shocked by the amount of devastation London had taken. Buzz bombs were still falling and V2 rocket bombs which wiped out a whole block of buildings had started to drop. London was taking a terrible beating.

While in London, I obtained my release from the British Merchant Navy and joined the Canadian Merchant Marine. I was repatriated to Canada on a P. @ O. vessel and then joined the **S/S Kawartha Park** and served on her until the end of the war with Germany. On November 25th, 1945, I signed off the **S/S Kawartha Park** and left the deep sea behind forever.

Epilogue

Ah, Love! Could thou and I
  with Fate conspire
To grasp this sorry Scheme
  of Things entire,
Would not we shatter it
  to bits-and then
Re-mould it nearer to the
  Heart's Desire!

(Rubaiyat of Omar Khayyam)

Weary of war and tired of always being a stranger in a strange land I felt that now I needed to get out into the fresh air and I bought a farm. It was about three miles from my father's farm near Galt, Ontario. My brother, Hugh; after getting out of the RCAF had returned and was running that farm. The soil on the farm we purchased proved none too productive; but I managed to improve it over the years and built up a good dairy herd.

I eventually sold the farm and headed west by car. As we reached Kelowna and saw the view above the bridge I said, 'This is as far as I will ever go and this will be my town."

Many years later during my retirement years I obtained a radio amateur call number and took up Ham radio communication as a hobby. My call number was VE7BSC and I "talked" with other Hams all over the world. Of course I was in the safety of my home and not in the ship's Radio Office!

A.K.M. Patterson Radio Officer—British Wireless Marine Service

Glossary

Muezzin—The Mohammedan Priest that calls the faithful to prayer from the Minaret of a Mosque

Fez(sing) Fezzes (Plu) Red Brimless hat worn by those of the Mohammedan faith in many parts of the east.

Brahminy Kites—The large rusty colored kites common to India.

Frangipanni—A tropical shrub with an insignificant looking green flower that is very fragrant and sweet selling Particularly on moonlight nights.

Marijuana—a drug made from the Indian Hemp plant (Cannabis Sativa) and is similar to hashish—first came to notice in Mexico.

Feluccas—Egyptian sailing boats with single sails

Rickisha—Two wheeled, man pulled vehicle common to India and far east.

Sinhalese or Cingalese—The Natives of Ceylon

Durian—An evil smelling fruit much appreciated by Chinese, Burmese, etc.
They claim that it has aphrodisiac powers

Dacoit—A Burmese bandit—dacoity—robbing

Gharry—Indian horse drawn vehicle(Garri) Hindustani

Bakshish—gift of money

Hibiscus—shrub common in Australia and West Indies, has red flowers.

About Alan

I am Alan's daughter Mahrie, and I have been thrilled to have the privilege of compiling his diaries about the British Merchant Marine and his travels through the East. This task of putting his words in print has been very revealing to me with new insight into Alan's thoughts and feelings. Alan used to tell me how very lucky he was as many times he would just get off one ship to transfer to another and the previous ship would be blown to bits! I still have his "lucky" Hindu Ganish carving that sat on his desk in each ship he ever served upon. He never went back to sea, but he did enjoy a 17 foot motor boat on the Okanagan Lake!

In his retirement years Alan again became *"The Radio Man"* as he joined an Amateur Radio club. His call numbers were VE7BSC. Some of you *"radio men"* out there may remember Alan. He was always a great communicator and I'm hoping that by publishing his diaries he will continue to be able to communicate and share his knowledge and rare sense of humor with anyone who is lucky enough to pick up and read this book. The short verse at the beginning of each of the seven parts to this book was taken from *"The Rubaiyat of Omar Khayyam"*. This book, written by an eleventh century Persian, was with Alan throughout the war years and it was one of his favorite books during that time.

This book is dedicated to Alan K. M. Patterson (VE7BSC) and to the British Merchant Marine Service

Signing on and off Various Ships

S.S. Mitchell—on Jan. 10th/38—Off Feb. 23/38

S.S. Marslew—on March 10th/38—off June 21/38 *(sunk in November of 1942)*

S.S. Contractor—on June 24th/38—off Aug. 10th/38

S.S Indora—on Aug. 10th/38—off Dec. 31/38—

S.S Indora—On Jan 1/39—off July 4th/39

S.S. Indora. On July 5th/39—Off Aug. 21st/39

S.S. Sir H. Adamson—on Aug. 22/39—Off Aug. 27th/39

S.S Indora—On Aug. 28th/39—off Sept. 18th/39

S.S. Indora—On Sept. 20th/39—off Nov. 30th/39

S.S. Indora—On Dec. 1/39—off March 7th/40

S.S. Indora—On March 8th/1940—Off April 13/1940

S.S. Indora—On April 14th/40—Off April 12th/41 *(sunk March 6th, 1942 by torpedoes)*

S.S Warina On April 24th/41—July 23/44 *(Scrapped in 1950)*

S/S Samspring—July 1944 home to the U.K. *(Scrapped in 1969)*

Obtained release from the British Merchant Marine and joined the Canadian Merchant Marine.

Information about Alan's ships

S.S. Mitchell
Owned by Douglas and Ramsey
Captain: Kelley
Tonnage (gross)-5510
Signed on Jan. 10/38 (New York) and off Feb. 23/38 (Rosyth, Scotland)

S.S. Marslew
Owners: Walmar Steamship Co
Call signal: GMPZ
Captain: Ferguson
Signed on Mar. 10/38 (Glasgow) and off on June 21, 1938 in Manchester

S.S. Contractor
Owners J@C Harrison
Call sig: GTNC
Captain Collins
Signed on June 24/38 in Liverpool and off Aug.9th, 1938 in Calcutta

S.S. Indora
Owners: British India Steam Nav.Co.
Call sig: GKGS—Official No 166382
Captain Wordingham and Johnson
Signed on Aug. 10–38 in Calcutta and off Aug. 22, 1939

S/S Sir Harvey Adamson
Owners: British India Steam Co.
Call sig: GRYK
Captain Taylor
Signed on Aug . 23, 1939 and off Aug. 27, 1939

S/S Indora
Captains: Johnson
Official No. 166382
Signed on Aug. 28, 1939 in Rangoon and off April 12th, 1941 in Rangoon

S/S Warina
Captain: Drummond
Official No. 142433 (Registered at London)
Signed on April 24th, 1941 at Rangoon and left for the hospital

Approximate Distances Traveled During 1938

New York U.S.A. To Rosyth, Scotland on S.S. Mitchell	3644 miles
Glasgow-Liverpool to Montevideo, Uruguay, Buenos Aires	6343 miles
River Plate Ports, Buenos Aires, Arg., to Manchester (Marslew)	6291 miles
Liverpool, England to Calcutta, India on S.s Contractor	7877miles
Calcutta to Colombo, Ceylon on S.S. Indora	1250 miles
Colombo to Calcutta, India	1250 miles
Rangoon to Kankesanturai, Ceylon	1100
Kankesanturai to Colombo, Ceylon	450
Colombo to Trivandrum, India	209
Trivamdrum to Allepei	75
Allepei to Cochin	34
Cochin to Bombay	585
Bombay to Tuticorin	740
Tuticorin to Calcutta	1300
Calcutta to Rangoon, Burma	779
Rangoon to Moulmein	150
Moumein to Calcutta, India	850
Calcutta to Rangoon, Burma	779
1938 Total Miles Traveled	**34485 miles**

Approximate Distances Traveled During 1939

Rangoon—Bombay-Bhavnagar-Veraval-Porebundar Bedi Bundar-Navalaki-Kutchkundla-Karachi on S.S. Indora	2,996
Karachi to Pondicherry, Fr. India	1861
Pondicherry to Bassein, Burma	946
Bassein to Rangoon	260
Rangoon-Colombo-Tuticorin-Quilon and Bombay	2,206
Bombay-Quilon-Colombo-Akyab, Burma	2,127
Akyab, Burma to Calcutta, India	404
Calcutta to Rangoon, Burma	779
Rangoon-Bombay-Bhavnagar-Bedibundar-Navlaki-Karachi	3,071
Karachi-Madras-Rangoon	2,909
Rangoon-Tavoy-Mergui @ back to Rangoon	668
Rangoon-Colombo-Bombay-Karachi	2,618
Karachi to Suez	2,800
Suez to Bombay	3,000
Bombay to Suez	3,000
Suez to Calcutta	4,856
Calcutta to Singapore	1,740
Singapore to Freemantle, Australia	2,313
1939 Total Miles Traveled	44,375

Approximate Distances Traveled in 1940

Freemantle, Australia to Adelaide	1,750 miles
Adelaide to Melbourne	535
Melbourne to Sydney	618
Sydney to Port Kembla	53
Port Kembla to Newcastle, Australia	116
New Castle to Sydney	72
Sydney to Hobart, Tasmania	666
Hobart to Melbourne	484
Melbourne to Adelaide	540
Adelaide to Freemantle	1,452
Freemantle to Colombo	3,169
Colombo-Trincomalee-Madras-Calcutta	1,481
Calcutta to Rangoon	779
Rangoon-Calcutta-Mauritius-Capetown Port-Of-Spain, Trinidad-Barbados-Kingston-Jamaica	12,481
Jamaica-Havana-Cuba—New Orleans, U.S.A.	1,371
New Orleans-Liverpool-Swansea, Wales	5,192
Swansea-Milford Haven-Durban, S.A.-Penang, Malaya	13, 378
Penang, Malaya to Calcutta, India	1309
Calcutta to Rangoon, Burma	779
Rangoon to Moulmein	157
Moulmein to bassein	311

Bassein to Rangoon	264
Rangoon to Colombo	1,263
Colombo to Cochin	307
1940 Total Miles Traveled	48,527 miles

Approximate Distances Traveled During 1941

Cochin to Bombay	596
Bombay-Quilon-Tuticorin-Colombo-Rangoon	2,275
Veraval-Karachi	2,942
Karachi-Colombo-Akyab	2,578
Akyab-Colombo	1,260
Colombo-Rangoon	1,300
Rangoon-Karachi-Bahrein-Rastanura (S.S. Warina)	3,681
Rastanura-Karachi	969
Karachi-Bombay	591
Bombay-Cochin	681
Cochin-bassein (Cochin, Colombo, Bombay)	1,594
Bassein-Colombo	1,252
Colombo-Cochin	347
Cochin-Bombay	585
Bombay-Cochin	585
Cochin-Tuticorin	155
Tuticorin-Colombo	240
Colombo-Madras Madras-Calcutta	1,350
Calcutta-Colombo	1,350
Colombo-Bombay	940

Bombay-Karachi   563

*** The rest of the year was not filled in and we can only guess what happened.

Rules of the Road—Two Steamships meeting

When both side lights you see ahead
Starboard your wheel and show your red

Two steamships passing-
Green to green or red to red
Perfect safety up ahead

Two steamships crossing (position of greatest danger)
If to your starboard red appear
It is your duty to keep clear
To act as judgment says is proper
To port—or starboard-back—or stop her!

All ships to keep a good look out-
Both in safety and in doubt
Always keep a good lookout
But when upon your port is seen
A steamship starboard light of green
There is not so much for you to do
For green to port keeps clear of you

In danger with no room to turn
Ease her! Stop her! Go astern.

(Merchant Marines used this poem as a memory aid during examinations)

BRITISH WIRELESS MARINE SERVICE

Joint Service Department of:
The Marconi International Marine Communication Co. Ltd.,
Radio Communication Company Ltd., and Marconi Sounding Device Co. Ltd.
Marconi Offices, Electra House, Victoria Embankment, London, W.C.2.

LONDON (Head Office).
Telegraphic Address : "THULIUM,
ESTRAND."
Telephone No. - Temple Bar 4321
(Extension 387)
EAST HAM (Inspection).
Telegraphic Address : "MARINYCOM,
EHAM."
Telephone No. - Grangewood 0885
BELFAST.
Telegraphic Address : "THULIUM."
Telephone No. - Belfast 5346
CARDIFF.
Telegraphic Address : "THULIUM."
Telephone No. - Cardiff 6601
FLEETWOOD.
Telegraphic Address : "THULIUM."
Telephone No. - Fleetwood 398
GLASGOW.
Telegraphic Address : "THULIUM."
Telephone No. - Central 4316
GRIMSBY.
Telegraphic Address : "THULIUM."
Telephone No. - Grimsby 4501
HULL.
Telegraphic Address : "THULIUM."
Telephone No. - Central 2429
LIVERPOOL.
Telegraphic Address : "THULIUM."
Telephone No. - Bank 6221
MILFORD HAVEN.
Telegraphic Address : "THULIUM."
Telephone No - Milford Haven 313
NEWCASTLE-ON-TYNE.
Telegraphic Address : "THULIUM."
Telephone No. - Central 27381
SOUTHAMPTON.
Telegraphic Address : "THULIUM."
Telephone No. - Southampton 4918
SWANSEA.
Telegraphic Address : "THULIUM."
Telephone No. - Swansea 5649

Liverpool

Date *26th June* 193*8*

Mr. *R R M Patterson*

Please note that you are required to
take duty as FIRST, ~~SECOND,~~ ~~THIRD,~~
WIRELESS OPERATOR on board the

s.s. *Contractor*

Brunswick Dock.

Please arrange, therefore, to sign the Articles of this
Ship accordingly at ~~Shipping Office~~
on board
on *Friday* the *26th June* at *10 am*, and
deliver this document to the Officials of the Shipping Company
as your authority for so doing.

At the time of signing on you must obtain from the Board
of Trade Official definite instructions regarding the date
and time you are required to join this vessel.

Remarks

S 84.   250 Bks.

BRITISH WIRELESS MARINE SERVICE

JS Smith
Depot Manager

BRITISH
WIRELESS MARINE SERVICE

Joint Service Department of

The MARCONI INTERNATIONAL MARINE COMMUNICATION CO., LTD.

RADIO COMMUNICATION CO., LTD,

and MARCONI SOUNDING DEVICE CO., LTD.

5, TEMPLE CHAMBERS,
6, OLD POST OFFICE STREET,
CALCUTTA.

Ref. C.,0.898/41.

Telegrams: Thulium, Calcutta.
Telephone: Calcutta 2696.

Date ___23rd April 1941.___

Memorandum from **The Superintendent.**

To

Mr. A. K. M. Patterson.
Radio Officer.
ex s.s. "Indora".
C/o Messrs. Mackinnon Mackenzie & Co., Ltd.
R A N G O O N.

We regret to learn from Messrs. Mackinnon Mackenzie & Co., Calcutta, that you have been obliged to enter hospital with depressed fracture of the skull, and hope that by the time this letter reaches you, you will be well on the way to recovery.

As it is necessary for us to report all entries into hospital to the London Office, will you please forward us the following particulars as early as possible.

1. Name of Hospital.
2. Date signed off articles.
3. Date entry into hospital.
4. Cause of entry.
5. Probable duration of detention in hospital.
6. Condition of health.
7. Name of the ward or room and what is the charge per day.

If your stay in hospital is likely to be prolonged, will you please forward us a report every Monday stating your condition and progress, to enable us to include it in our Weekly hospital report to London. Also please let me know whether you desire your allotment (if any) cancelled, as you understand that with the exception of half pay during the first fortnight you are entitled to no salary whilst on sick leave.

Please return the enclosed Next of Kin form (in duplicate) duly completed.

Some of the "Gang"
S.S Mitchell

S.S. Mitchell   at
Portland, Maine

Looking forward from the bridge

These elephants handle heavy teak logs and Timbers with ease and are guided by the mahout who sits on their back.

They handle long planks with skill.

They use their feet when necessary to push a plank along.

Ships unloading cargo into Indian barges at Calcutta.
The Contractor is moored to the buoys in the
River Ganges.

Unloading Cargo at Trivandrum, India

#1 - S.S. Contractor

#2- Hindu bathing ghats, Ganges River

#3- Calcutta City Center

#4. Victoria Memorial modeled after the Taj Mahal, Agra.

#5 - Indian Sepoys on parade (soldiers)

These Jungle Burmese use round stone instead of arrows and are quite skillful at shooting birds.

Some of our hunters and our guide saw chief Hlaing the sub-inspector of Police eating their curry.

Truly East!
Karachi

Burmese Temple- Bassein

Moulmein, Burma

In from the desert

The Famous Shwedagon Pagoda (Rangoon)

The " Bloomin' Earthen Idol"
Bassein, Burma

The 3rd officer and self (Alan)
at the Shwe Dgon Pagoda

Enjoying her Cheroot

Here we are!

Karachi -Just in from the desert

Street corner in Calcutta

978-0-595-47022-8
0-595-47022-X